"Five words came to mind as I read t   ne
the entire book: fresh, suggestive, reflective, penetrating, and lasting. In *Becoming Curious*, spiritual formation is approached from an angle I've never seen: curiosity. Each chapter is question based enough to open up suggestions that led me constantly to reflection. At times the reflections became deeply penetrating, and as I have lived with *Becoming Curious*, the book lasts. You might put *Becoming Curious* back on your shelf, but don't be fooled: it will come back in odd moments to further reflection."

Scot McKnight, Julius R. Mantey Professor of New Testament, Northern Seminary

"The word that keeps coming to mind as I read *Becoming Curious* is 'humility.' Casey Tygrett invites us onto the path of Christlike humility in such a winsome and humble way. But don't mistake it for simplistic or shallow. There is a profound wisdom on every page that feels hard fought and God given—and these depths can only be received by humble curiosity. This book will change you if you let it."

Aaron Niequist, worship leader

"There is no one better than Casey Tygrett to ask the penetrating questions that will bring about the life Jesus truly wants us all to have. In *Becoming Curious*, Casey invites us into a life that focuses more on asking better questions than finding better answers. Join Casey as he teaches us how to stay curious and transforming in our lives with Christ."

Tim Harlow, senior pastor, Parkview Christian Church, Orland Park, Illinois, author of *Life on Mission*

"My friend Casey Tygrett not only gives us permission to become curious disciples, he shows us why it matters and how to do it. Beautiful! Casey's singular objective is to ignite our minds with Jesus' invitation into a life of kingdom curiosity. Majestic! I wholeheartedly recommend this book."

J. K. Jones, pastor of spiritual formation, Eastview Christian Church, coauthor of *We Speak*

"This book is filled with possibility, opportunity, and adventure. Casey's passion for the church is inspiring and his care for God's people is infectious. I love what he is calling us to. Read this book and refresh your soul!"

Naeem Fazal, Mosaic Church

"In a world that is brimming with redemptive potential, *Becoming Curious* winsomely invites us to receive the fullness of every moment. Humble curiosity is the gateway to formation, to learning and swimming into the deeper streams of faith. Casey masterfully shows through Scripture and story how the art of curiosity can form us more into Christlikeness. Profoundly thankful for this book!"

Steve Carter, teaching pastor, Willow Creek, author of *This Invitational Life*

"When I started reading *Becoming Curious*, I had intended to finish it over the span of a week. I finished it in one day! My friend Casey Tygrett has given us quite a gift in this book. You will find it a resource that will help you and others grow in faith and love. Be prepared to be encouraged, challenged, and strengthened."

Caleb Kaltenbach, lead pastor, Discovery Church, author of *Messy Grace*

"Questions are rarely allowed to linger in the air for too long before someone feels compelled to answer them. Rather than let our curiosity lead us more deeply into understanding God or one another, we rush to certainties and supposed sure things. In *Becoming Curious*, Casey Tygrett reclaims the transformational power of a curious question for the faithful, encouraging believers to do what may seem counterintuitive in our culture—to ask another question rather than find a quick answer. While reading this book, I had the distinct feeling that Casey crafted these words with great humility in his heart and a smile in his eyes—the kind that only comes from a man who has released his right to know everything and rests well in the presence of Jesus. Casey Tygrett is one of my new favorite authors, and *Becoming Curious* is an anthem of hope for believers who have grown tired of well-oiled religion."

Emily P. Freeman, *Wall Street Journal*–bestselling author of *Simply Tuesday*

becoming
curious

A SPIRITUAL PRACTICE
OF ASKING QUESTIONS

Casey Tygrett

Foreword by James Bryan Smith

IVP Books

An imprint of InterVarsity Press
Downers Grove, Illinois

InterVarsity Press
P.O. Box 1400, Downers Grove, IL 60515-1426
ivpress.com
email@ivpress.com

InterVarsity Press® is the book-publishing division of InterVarsity Christian Fellowship/USA®, a movement of students and faculty active on campus at hundreds of universities, colleges, and schools of nursing in the United States of America, and a member movement of the International Fellowship of Evangelical Students. For information about local and regional activities, visit intervarsity.org.

All Scripture quotations, unless otherwise indicated, are taken from THE HOLY BIBLE, NEW INTERNATIONAL VERSION®, NIV® Copyright © 1973, 1978, 1984, 2011 by Biblica, Inc.™ Used by permission. All rights reserved worldwide.

While any stories in this book are true, some names and identifying information may have been changed to protect the privacy of individuals.

Cover design: Cindy Kiple
Interior design: Daniel van Loon
Images: © David Keochkerian / Trevillion Images

ISBN 978-0-8308-4627-6 (print)
ISBN 978-0-8308-9249-5 (digital)

Printed in the United States of America ♾

Library of Congress Cataloging-in-Publication Data

Names: Tygrett, Casey, 1977- author.
Title: Becoming curious : a spiritual practice of asking questions / Casey
*   Tygrett ; foreword by James Bryan Smith.*
Description: Downers Grove : InterVarsity Press, 2017. | Includes
*   bibliographical references.*
Identifiers: LCCN 2017000164 (print) | LCCN 2017007799 (ebook) | ISBN
*   9780830846276 (pbk. : alk. paper) | ISBN 9780830892495 (eBook)*
Subjects: LCSH: Spiritual life--Christianity. | Questioning. | Curiosity.
Classification: LCC BV4501.3 .T94 2017 (print) | LCC BV4501.3 (ebook) | DDC
*   248.4--dc23*
LC record available at https://lccn.loc.gov/2017000164

P	22	21	20	19	18	17	16	15	14	13	12	11	10	9	8	7	6	5	4	3	2	1
Y	36	35	34	33	32	31	30	29	28	27	26	25	24	23	22	21	20	19	18	17

To Holley and the B,

because we always play as a team.

And to everyone else on the journey of becoming.

Journey on.

contents

foreword

JAMES BRYAN SMITH

As I write this foreword, our home is in the middle of a massive renovation. The entire main floor has been taken down to the studs and is slowly being rebuilt. We live in an older home, and that usually means you run into a lot of surprises. We certainly have. Those surprises usually involve more costs and delaying the project. It certainly has. One evening, just as the workers were about to leave, I peered through an opening cut in the floor. Beneath it was a crawl space. I saw a reflection. I got a flashlight and looked down. There was water. I dropped a rock down and heard a *plop*. The water was four inches deep, in a crawl space of around 150 square feet. I felt a pit in my stomach. The worker said to me, "This isn't good." The foreman came over and walked me through ways to solve the problem. They all cost more money and would delay the project.

After he left, I walked around the entire main floor and stopped to look at everything that had gone wrong. With each pace my frustration increased. Over and over I muttered, "Why did we do this project? We should have listed it." An hour later my wife, Meghan, came home. She had been gone a few days. I took her to the crawl space, and showed her the water. She calmly said, "Well, we just have to get it fixed." Then she looked up to see the progress that had been made. The "open concept" was finally opened, and she could see what it was going to look like. She smiled and said, "Isn't this beautiful?" I said, "No, it's awful, and this whole project has been a disaster." She disagreed.

"Remember the day we walked into this home? We both turned to each other and said, 'My soul feels right in this house. Let's make it our home.' We love this home. Let's keep on loving it."

The next day I began reading this book.

By the time I had finished, something inside of me had changed: my *attitude*. I walked down to the main floor and looked at the space with new eyes. I was not upset or frustrated. I looked at every nook and cranny with curiosity and wonder. I saw possibilities, not problems. I wondered about the history of the home. I knew it was built in 1940. I thought about what life was like for the builders and for the family that first inhabited it. America had not yet entered WWII. I wondered if they were nervous about the state of the world, if they or someone they knew fought in the war. Having thought about the past, I began to think about our future in this house.

I walked into each space with curiosity about the future. What conversations would be held here? I imagined the space filled with laughter, the smells of delicious food, and quiet evenings by the fireplace. I imagined one day meeting my children's future spouses, and my future grandchildren coming into this space. I imagined them saying, "Wow, this is beautiful!" The place was transfigured. I was on sacred ground. I could feel it. I smiled.

I love it when I read those rare books that forever change you. For me, some of those books include C. S. Lewis's *Mere Christianity*, Richard Foster's *Celebration of Discipline*, Dallas Willard's *The Divine Conspiracy*, St. Teresa's *Interior Castle*, and Hans Urs von Balthasar's *Love Alone Is Credible*. The one in your hands is now added to the list. It disarmed me. It humbled me. It exposed the absurdity of need for control, and created a longing in me to become as a child on Christmas morning or at Disney World. It reminded me that Christianity is *not* about dogma or doctrine or rules. Christianity is based on a magnificent Story that we get to enter. It is about entering the true Magic Kingdom, an interactive life with the Author of the Story.

This book will teach you how to see the world with childlike wonder, give you boldness to ask God for what you want, confirm your identity in Christ, and help you see the *why* of your life, not just the what and the how. It will help you to see others in a new way, to embrace even your failures, to rewire the way you think about rituals, and to increase your ability to forgive and to raise questions. But what I most want to say to you is this: let this book help you to embrace the gift of curiosity.

Casey Tygrett is a fine man, passionate pastor, and a very good writer. This book had the power to lift my spirit in the midst of discouraging circumstances. It reminded me that I need to let go of my expectations, my plans, and my desires in order to see the world afresh and aglow with the grandeur of God. So I commend the wise purchase of this book, and I leave you with a benediction written by Larry Hein:

May all your expectations be frustrated.

May all your plans be thwarted.

May all your desires be withered into nothingness.

That you may experience the powerlessness and poverty of a child and sing, dance, and trust in the love of God who is Father, Son, and Spirit.

Amen.

introduction

He has been waiting all year for this very moment.

The cold of the house is strong, the light-streaked wood floors creaking with every step as a little boy creeps toward the warm light of the family room.

Put this boy (or girl)—wrinkled pajamas and reddened cheeks—in your mind. Remember when you were there, aching for what you think you know, but don't know. Remember all the assumptions, desires, hopes, and fears of all the years that would hopefully be met under the tree that day.

To be sure, Christmas morning comes differently to children.

Children come wide open and breathless, while adults are grasping for the coffee and cameras, handling all the details. Children dive foolishly into the packages as if no one is watching. Adults look for a trash bag, trying to bring order out of the chaos. Kids give little thought to what their flourish looks like to others, they only hope for what might be waiting.

They want to *know*. They want to tear through that paper and satisfy their curiosity.

What will it be like?

What will it feel like to hold it?

Will it be everything I hoped?

The child pulls back the papery veil and sees the gift, eyes twitching with the realization that what he had wondered and curiously considered for all the days prior was now, ironically, *present*. The gift had been chosen—carefully and specifically for him—the tags cut off, gift receipts stashed away in a drawer in the off chance that it wasn't the right color or size. This gift, this day, there is no need for returns. The gift fits the anticipation and desire, and so the boy begins to glow.

Suddenly, the moment is alive with potential: *What can I do with this now?*

From Christmas to Crossroads

In every country, in every place, a gift says you are loved and valued. A gift reaffirms your place as worthy of grace, worthy of gratuity. You are worthy to be received and loved at the core of your being. This is true of God's gifts to us as well.

The gifts of God seem relatively easy to find in the pages of Scripture: gifts like grace in spite of our performance (Romans 5:15), a life with the scent of eternity (Romans 6:23), skills and abilities that give divine texture to our world (1 Corinthians 2:12), and even our specific purpose for walking in the world (1 Timothy 4:14).

Finding the gifts is easy, but it's the next question that matters most: What changes in my everyday life—in the very contours of my soul— when I hold these gifts, feeling them light yet strong in my hands?

In the pages of this book I have one particular gift from God I want to offer to you. It is wrapped and somewhat hidden, causing us to tilt our heads like a Labrador retriever when we gaze at it. It waits for our courage—our spiritual bravery—to take it by the sides and begin to tear the thin paper at the edges.

It is the spiritual practice of becoming curious.

Why the Gift of Curiosity?

There's a difficult line to walk between what we need to know and what falls into the realm of mystery. Walking that line often wears on our nerves and causes incredible tension, and so we settle for easy answers. We stop asking questions. We give up. We begin to lose the one thing that fiercely energizes the transformation of our souls—something beautiful, poetic, joyful, and happily disruptive: *curiosity*.

Curiosity is essential to movement in our lives.

A little curiosity moves us deeper into the lives of our children and friends.

A little curiosity helps us understand strange emotions and where they are coming from.

A little curiosity helps us find opportunities and graces for life we never knew existed.

A little curiosity, especially when we're chasing Jesus, will shape and form us into the person he calls us to be.

We have to learn to be curious again in our journey with Jesus.

For me, curiosity hasn't always been a welcome companion. For a pastor and teacher, typically the emphasis is on expertise—the goal of belief and faith is knowledge and the dispersion of that knowledge to others. Pastors or teachers who receive glowing reviews usually do so because they always had *the right word to say* or *knew what someone needed to hear*. They had some kind of advanced understanding, and that understanding made them good, great, or amazing, depending on the situation.

When we combine seminaries that often take an academic approach to Scripture through Enlightenment educational theory with the somewhat militant approach evangelical Christianity has taken to apologetics, it's not hard to see how curiosity gets moved to the margins.

Questions and curiosities, especially those we can't nail down, are signs of weakness in a debate. God says it, we believe it, and that settles it—no questions asked.

I was mentored in this kind of faith: the path of answering people's questions and being the "wise sage." Then I started failing at sagehood, and it began to tear away at my soul.

But what if there wasn't a big fish who swallowed Jonah?

What about all that violence in the Old Testament?

Why is Jesus so different from Paul?

Is there space to believe, even with these questions?

If I couldn't be "right" or at least have all these questions buttoned up, then what was the state of my soul? I began to discover that as we walk in skin we eventually find that the moment we believe we are standing firm, the wind begins to howl, threatening our equilibrium. Not the dark night of the soul, per se, but more like the falling dusk of uncertainty.

As I began to engage my own curiosity in following Jesus, I encountered questions in myself, my friends, and our community that I could not answer. Instead of rushing to end the suspense, I found instead that the deep yearning of my spirit was actually to leave them unanswered. It felt counterintuitive, counterproductive. There had to be a different way, but to chase it would be to go back on everything I had already learned.

A Question of Change

The other gift that came into my life around this time was the gift of *change*. Aging, growing in a bit of wisdom as I tried to cultivate space for the living and radical Jesus in my comings and goings, I saw my convictions begin to change. Slowly, I learned that for God to grant new mercies every morning (Lamentations 3:22-23) my soul had to take the shape of an explorer—a daily searcher coming to know old things in a new way.

It takes discipline to live like that, and a deep trust that Jesus guides and directs even when the wind of change is swirling in our spirits. As I lived, taught others, and engaged in spiritual conversations, I began to think, *What if my best answer to someone's question regarding God or faith is to ask another question, the one just below the surface?*

I now imagine Jesus replying, "Yes, precisely."

Becoming curious then is a process of change, of *return*—going back to the fundamentals of our own lives and existence. Seth Godin says that becoming curious is "more about a five-, ten- or fifteen-year process where you start finding your voice, and finally you begin to realize that the safest thing you can do feels risky and the riskiest thing you can do is play it safe."

Curiosity is not for the faint-hearted; it is for the God-haunted and restless spirits dying for the water just below the surface of earthly certainty.

Is it possible that if we take this path, pursuing curiosity through Jesus, we may find that instead of walking a straight line this pilgrimage with God is actually a tight and imperceptible spiral that brings us back around to the beginning only to learn new things again?

Curious, isn't it? That is my hope for this book. To ignite our minds with possibilities. What if Jesus actually wanted us to grow and deepen in our curiosity, more than our certainty or our knowledge of facts and data?

More than that, what if Jesus himself instigated the chase after questions like some sort of wise and loving prankster, planting little explosive ideas that when they combusted produced fruit and not fractures? What would it look like for us to create space—practice a spiritual discipline daily or weekly—where we gave ourselves permission to not know and to simply *ask* things of Jesus?

What to Expect

This book is meant to be a conversation, taking a look at the questions surrounding Jesus with an eye toward how they change us, shaping our souls for authentic living in a world where certainty comes and goes like the weather. As Michael Hidalgo says, "God is the same yesterday, today and forever but yesterday and today are not the same at all." The world is constantly changing, and so the way we walk with Jesus in a changing world is open to change as well.

As I started writing this book I began the practice of keeping a questions journal. I have to confess that I didn't keep up with the journal for a consecutive period of days; some days were more fruitful than others, however the purpose was to force myself to deal with the kind of questions that were pressing at that very moment. I am surprised even now to go back and read some of the entries.

During the time when I was writing that journal, our congregation experienced two devastating events: we lost a young, newlywed woman, and our friends' daughter was rushed to the pediatric ICU in Orlando, Florida, for what would be the beginning of a seventy-day hospital experience. Peppered among the queries that arose during these two deeply challenging moments were garden-variety doubts and uncertainties about God and the darkness in my own mind about death, curiosity about writing and vocation, as well as musings about my relationships. In other words, when we open the door to questions and curiosity, things flow out that we don't expect.

At the end of each chapter you'll have a chance to engage the discipline of curiosity by using your own questions journal. The habit and practice of writing down your own curious questions as you read through the reflections on the questions of Jesus will stoke the fires of curiosity in your own life. I hope this practice will get us into the habit of asking good and beautiful questions rather than passively settling for someone else's certainty or faking our own certainty when it becomes a thin paper sheath over our hearts and minds.

Before we go any further, there are three distinct gifts that I pray this book will give you as you read.

The Gift of Permission

Imagine that you've just started a new job. You don't know much about your boss other than what your coworkers have said in passing, but you do know you want to keep this job as long as possible. Sometime in the first few weeks, you figure out that your boss made a huge mistake that could reflect badly on you. What do you do? Do you go to your boss and bring this up? How will the boss react? What will be the consequences? Should you unpack those boxes of supplies or keep them handy in case you're shown the door?

Too often this is our picture of God. Therefore, to ask questions or to pose challenges seems out of line, disobedient, or disrespectful. And we're afraid to get a comeback from God much like Job did: "Will the one who contends with the Almighty correct him?" (Job 40:2).

If God doesn't want our challenges or questions, then we'll need to stop reading (and I'll stop writing) right now. We can also cut most of the psalms out of our Bibles. After that, the challenge becomes: Where else do we take these concerns, questions, uncertainties, and cloudiness? Is it possible that the curiosities the Bible poses are invitations to bring our own curiosities to the text?

If we see anything in Jesus, it is both the permission and the invitation to bring our questions and uncertainties to him—to sit with them together, to meditate and examine in the presence of One who loves us and holds us up. The hope is that questions from the mouth of Jesus himself will give you the permission to ask what has been haunting you, occupying your thoughts and feelings.

The Gift of Tension

Jesus told his disciples, "[your Father in heaven] makes his sun rise on the evil and on the good, and sends rain on the righteous and on the unrighteous" (Matthew 5:45 NRSV). You could have heard the crickets chirping for *miles* after Jesus said this.

How could God give rain—the thing that makes crops grow and gives life to a people who are living off the land—to those who are not righteous? How could he give the beautiful sun to those who are evil? These are beautiful, curious questions. For a time and space like today where we are overwhelmed by sound bites and talking heads, we need these kinds of questions because they introduce the gift of *tension*.

Tension means, "being held in a state between two or more forces which are acting in opposition to each other." Tension is when a good God gives bad, evil, unrighteous farmers the rain and sun they need. Tension makes us think. Tension makes us ask questions. Tension erases the boundaries between *us* and *them*, because with God everyone is part of the "us."

Tension is a huge part of curiosity because asking a question throws open a multitude of possibilities, both known and unknown. As we'll see later, this is precisely the kind of tension involved in discovering the kingdom Jesus so often proclaimed. We instead confess that someone else might have the answer, or at least we're willing to put our long-held assumption under the microscope and curiously examine it to see what God may have to say.

Frankly, we don't like tension. We like uncertainty even less, and as a matter of fact we see uncertainty as a hidden sin, a dark and sinister root that will destroy us. We ignore that Jesus consistently and compassionately cultivates tension. He asks questions and then doesn't answer them, feeding uncertainty. Perhaps Jesus isn't as scared of the sinister root as we are. Maybe he knows something we don't.

The point is that the reflections and questions in this book may cause you to feel tension. They may question texts that you have long since made up your mind about. Please sit for a moment, prayerfully and quietly, with that tension. Don't abandon it right off the bat. Tension can be good. Besides, tension is the smoke from curiosity's fire; where you find one, there is always the other.

The Gift of Rest

As a pastor and follower of Jesus, I find that the further I go the more questions I have. With seminary degrees and solid Bible study tools,

I still find myself wrestling with the questions and actions of the mysterious Messiah of the Bible. Perhaps you are there too. Perhaps you've felt exhausted by the curiosity, exhausted by trying to lift "clear texts" out of Scripture and apply them to the present shifting moments without the least bit of tension or challenge.

Perhaps you're feeling led to a worship style, community, or doctrinal position that was at one point out of the question and even *evil* to you. I understand, I've been there. And, frankly, as I write this sentence *I am there*.

I believe Jesus' response to us is "rest." Take the comforting words of Jesus to "find rest for your souls" (Matthew 11:29) and realize that the same Jesus who calls to comfort also catalyzes our curiosity with his very words and actions.

So let your curiosity be a good thing, a blessing, even if it doesn't feel good to you at the moment. Be content in it, knowing that these trials are the things that shape us more than anything else in the world (see Romans 5:3-5).

If we rest with the curious rabbi Jesus, who asked more questions than he answered, I believe we will walk forward in wisdom when our fellow travelers have lost their way.

And now, the first question: *Are you curious?*

Then let's begin.

CHAPTER ONE

why curiosity matters

When trees are waving wildly in the wind, one group of people
thinks that it is the wind that moves the trees; the other group
thinks that the motion of the trees creates the wind.

G. K. CHESTERTON

Why are we often
uneasy with curiosity?

What is so troubling about our curiosities, our questions? What about our wondering, pondering, and investigating? Aren't they very normal pieces of our everyday life?

Every day we are alive, every breathing moment, we are asking questions. Some of these daily questions are settled to a certain extent, answered, and we move on. Sometimes we leave them and move on out of frustration. Then, the day ends and we revisit the questions again. Afresh. Anew.

What will happen today?

What will come of this conversation, this meeting, this unending series of challenges?

Why am I wrestling again with the same challenges and destructive habits?

Am I really loved and accepted by those around me?

What can I do to make up for wounding that person in my life?

While working on this book I was also exchanging emails with a friend who had many questions about this journey of faith. She had questions about the Bible, about how all of the things that Christian traditions claim could possibly be true, and about the very interesting relationship between the God of the Old Testament and the Jesus of the New.

They do seem strikingly different, don't they?

When I mentioned that I was writing a book about spiritual formation and curiosity, she asked that I remember that curiosity is also a way of dealing with *doubt*.

Yes. However, I wonder if sometimes doubt—doubt that troubles the faithful and even disconnects people from a journey of faith—is simply curiosity cast as a villain? Where else do we find the language to process doubt, mystery, struggle, and even uncertainty if we have no space for curiosity?

Doubt can be wonder, exploration, or the engagement of a God-wired brain in its highest gear. How can something we're wired to do become antithetical to being faithful rather than the sweetness and energy of faith itself? Why do Christian communities attach fault or failure to strong currents of curiosity?

The reality is that curiosity does not have a favorable track record in the history of Christian tradition. The church throughout history has responded to curiosity in ways that make us cringe today.

Galileo curiously questioned the earth's position in the galaxy, and his answer was threats of execution.

Martin Luther wondered what repentance really meant—whether it was the prescription for a set of rituals or a movement of mind and heart—and he was put on trial.

Jesus asked . . .

What *did* Jesus ask?

I believe this question is the key to curiosity having a chance to shape and form us in our journey with Jesus. If spiritual formation is going to have any impact on how we live our daily lives, it has to reveal Jesus as one who gives space to the curious questions of we pilgrims.

The whole discussion starts with an announcement: Jesus' first great announcement, to be specific.

The Big Picture

First words are important.

The first thing you say when you go on a date can make or break the future of the relationship.

My wife will tell you that our first date was, to be mild, *underwhelming*. We went to a mediocre restaurant, she had to pay because I had no financial resources at the time, and the meal included chicken fingers. Yes, fried chicken fingers.

Not exactly *The Notebook*.

Thankfully she stuck with me, but if she'd had higher expectations for that night or if she had only a mild interest in being with me, we likely would have gone our separate ways. First things are fragile, and first words can be dangerous.

Jesus' first impression was unique because it came in the form of a bold and ambitious announcement: "Repent, for the kingdom of heaven has come near" (Matthew 3:2).

For much of my life, and perhaps yours, the word *repent* has come across with a pointed finger and a disgusted scowl, as if Jesus has "had it up to here" with me. I can't hear the word *repent* without thinking of fire-and-brimstone preachers from my past using it like a verbal meat cleaver to separate sinners from their wayward paths.

If we ask a few questions and listen to what's behind the word *repent*, a few things start to appear. For example, the audience for Jesus' teaching on repentance was largely Jewish, people who already were *technically* God's people.

How do you repent when you're already part of the fabric of God's great tapestry? This is why it was so troubling for me to hear the command "repent" as a teenager in the middle of the sweltering heat of a summer revival service. I was certain I had covered that ground already.

The people Jesus spoke to weren't surprised either. Prophets had been saying for years that the people of God must turn from worshiping wood-and-stone gods and instead would trust him to make good on his promise.

Jesus was doing something different though.

The Invitation

A few months ago I was on an airplane, and since everything I had brought to occupy myself on the flight required an electronic device, I had some time on my hands as we went nose-first into the clouds.

I pulled out the in-flight magazine and noticed an ad that said, "Fly [airline]."

Maybe I'm the only one who reads things this way, but I noticed that it was phrased as a *command*. English-language experts will say this sentence is in the imperative voice. That's the *command* voice. That's the "parent" voice, if we're talking to our children.

Look both ways.

Eat your veggies.

Get out of the cookie dough.

When Jesus says "repent," it sounds a lot like "parent" voice. If you look at the original Greek word, bingo, it appears Jesus is going into Dad mode.

Imperative.

Repent.

I'm not asking, I'm *telling* you.

So back to the in-flight magazine: Should I have felt like the airline was giving me a command from on high? Honestly, I was already on that particular airline's plane, so I didn't need to be ordered around. Who did they think they were? But the thought occurred to me: *Why don't I feel like someone's ordering me around when I read this?*

The reason is that sometimes the imperative is a command, and sometimes it's an *invitation*.

It takes some curiosity to unravel whether we're hearing a direct command or an invitation because the line between the two isn't always stark and clean. But what if there is something deep and good in finding that difference?

Or, if we really want to stir things up, what if *all* of Jesus' imperatives are *invitations*? If people are already seeking God, walking with him in whatever way they may find, then what happens when they hear "repent" as an invitation and not a command?

What if "repent" is actually the embossed invitation to a grand meal spread on a majestic table?

What if "repent" is the key to us walking backwards into our own story of trial, faith, and doubt, and seeing it all differently for the first time?

What if "repent" is not about the threat of hell or damnation, but instead it is the call to be *formed* differently?

What if "repent" means we see every teaching and action of Jesus as an invitation, and learn to ask question upon question about what that looks like in our story today?

What if "repent" is learning how to see the damp cloak of doubt as curiosity in disguise?

To repent means "a change of mind." The word both in Hebrew and in Greek affects thought *and* action—they are "head and hand" words. Literally, they mean to "turn one's head" and "return" to where you've come from. Repentance then is both a once and a daily move of our whole soul toward God. It is a learning, unlearning, and relearning kind of journey.

If we read Jesus' great announcement in this light, it sounds like this: "Come and think about things differently, because God's plan and desires are coming to life right now."

What can ordinary people do with that?

Converting Again and Again

The work and movement of God in ordinary people, the way we follow Jesus every moment of every day, is the great project of creating space for God to get his way in us. It surprises us and reimagines the way we see everything: from church to politics to sex to our social media presence.

That's why he began with *repent*. Rethink. Reimagine. Relearn.

In Jesus' time this relearning process was a necessity. Jesus' walking in the world was a way of reimagining everything. The Jewish religious leaders and their people had expectations based on the wise texts of their ancestors who had also walked with God.

There would be a kingdom. A King. A new temple would be built, and a people would be brought back together under the Jewish law, the rich and holy instructions of God.

There would be peace, yes, far-reaching peace. The vicious Romans who occupied the land would be, ahem, moved off, and there would finally be safety and prosperity.

The vision of this kind of kingdom is what most of us live with every day, with or without Jesus. We transpose this vision onto what we believe about God, or we may take the mantle of "king" on ourselves and then forge our way toward peace, safety, and security on our own "lands." We are built for a kingdom, one way or the other.

We build our territory, our castle, and our treasure, and eventually we find out that being king is both exhausting and beyond our pay grade.

There are too many questions for us to answer, so we get lost in the details. Or we settle for the easy and pragmatic answers and attempt to take the world by force.

In either case, we are far from what Jesus had in mind for the kingdom. He was a king, yes, but one with a very different vision of the kingdom. Could he in fact be the King if he had a different way of fulfilling the kingdom?

Could it be a kingdom of generosity instead of accumulation?

Could it be a kingdom made up of both those we'd put on the guest list and those we'd refuse to associate with?

Could it be a kingdom that both lives within national borders and has a worldwide influence?

Repenting Through Questions

To live in that kingdom would require something to shift in people. It would require our hearts, minds, and hands to be shaped for different work even within the glorious and grotesque circumstances we live in.

The kingdom requires new, curious questions.

We can't simply think the same and act differently. No, Jesus' invitation to repent is essential to shaping our lives for a way of living an old-kingdom promise with a new-world script.

What if Jesus' vision of the kingdom had to be run through the strainer created by years of our wandering and self-reliance? What if the way the kingdom of God explodes into our lives actually respects the little details of what has happened in our lives up to this point? He may choose to redeem them, to remove them, to take them like a potter pulls misshapen clay off of the wheel and begin to reshape them into something new.

In either story, ours or the people of Israel's, there is a need to ask some new questions and cultivate a new vision based on what is happening now and what glorious possibilities may come in the future.

Jesus, and now his Spirit that lives within us (John 14:17, 25), longs to shape us for a world within a world, and it is one that requires rediscovering our curiosity.

Why do I believe this?

The Curious King

Jesus changed the story by asking questions. He didn't do it by command, though Jesus gave commandments. He didn't do it by debate, though Jesus could hold his own when the situation merited it.

Jesus in the Gospels engages with nearly 183 questions. Sometimes he asks, sometimes he's responding, but what I can't shake is that in the nearly three years Jesus had to transform the narrative of the people of God he often chose to ask *instead* of tell.

Jesus' questions are amazing:

Why do you call me "good"?

What's in the Law, how do you read it?

What are you talking about as you walk along?

Who was a neighbor to the man beaten by the roadside?

Where are your accusers?

From time to time he doesn't answer the specific question at all and instead tells a story that answers a question no one had even *thought of,* much less asked.

Why do you break the actual law to ruthlessly keep the traditions and interpretations of your elders?

The Jesus who changed the world shifted the narrative of God and humans, and he did it by *engaging curiosity.* The point of Jesus' questions was to stoke curiosity rather than seeing it as an obstacle or a problem. He was intentional, clever, honest, and persistent with every question he asked. He invited people to explore and think along with him saying, "If you have ears, listen deeply to this one."

How have we missed this beautiful gift?

The Curiosity Killer

Perhaps as you've been reading you have felt this tension rising in you. It started in your stomach and has now moved to your throat.

Curiosity brings uncertainty. The world is already too unstable and uncertain. Besides, aren't there truths that we don't need to question?

Let's face it: easy answers are better than curiosity because they are aptly named. They're easy. Curiosity is hard, and that's why we often miss the gift within the questions.

A desire for certainty is understandable. I feel it even now as I write this. I want my story to be formed around predictable characters—friends who are after my good as much as I'm after theirs, churches that act responsibly with their authority and resources, and governments that really represent the best interests of their people.

My want for certainty in my story, that predictability and stability, flows out of the reality that none of the details are promised.

Friends, churches, and governments will fail and *do* fail. Beyond that, I will fail. I'm not a certainty in the story of others either. I want to be, desperately, and the rhythms and habits of my life with Jesus are built to tell that story in bold print. Yet I'm not always a certainty.

Sometimes uncertainty is good. None of us want change, but age and stage demand that we change. We ask new questions as we walk into new areas of our lives—from our parent's house to out on our own, from married to single, from single and dating to single and settled, from able-bodied and energetic to slow and steady in our latter days.

I began asking some soul-harrowing, habit-breaking, sleep-disrupting questions when I turned thirty-eight. What had I accomplished? What about these new aches and pains? What did I believe now, and why was it so different from what I held to before? Things long accepted became uncertain because new things were coming to mind.

Peter Greer and Greg Lafferty say, "That's the bewildering side of forty. Things you once considered unthinkable become powerfully appealing. If nothing else, anticipate it."

How can we approach the moments when things are shifting, when the unthinkable becomes appealing, if we don't have a curious habit that allows us to anticipate it? If our spirits immediately panic when questions arise in new ages and stages, we shouldn't be surprised when our decisions and emotions are hurried and destructive. It takes practice, cultivation, and familiarity with our curiosity to ask new questions about an old kingdom coming in a new way, filled with deep and beautiful secrets.

In my thoughts on getting older, I had to wrestle with this: if Jesus can't walk with us when we change through age and experience, and if we can't safely ask new and curious questions with him, then we have to wonder if Jesus is sufficient to address the reality of being human and being alive.

No Experts

The reason our development in curiosity matters is that in human development we come to a place where we feel supremely—sometimes foolishly—confident in our thoughts, practices, and ways of dealing with the world. We all desire competence in life, whether for our own health or for the approval of others.

I've got this.

I know what to do.

It isn't a negative thing for me to be able to handle parts of my own life. If I suddenly become completely incompetent in my personal hygiene, driving a car, or managing the very specific details of my job, that is probably going to be an issue.

The bigger problem is that we become supremely confident on *every* issue. Our fruitful study leads us to believe we're experts: we never miss the point, we never limit what we see by our own personal lenses or experiences, and we never *ever* get it wrong. To be wrong, we come to believe, is to be a failure.

Truly, we like to be around experts, people who know what they're doing. We'd like to *be* experts. People who have all the questions answered, so to speak. People who are certain, clear, and direct. Experts never fail to know the right answer to every question.

Which is why Jesus made a significant statement by inviting twelve fairly inexperienced, incompetent, and confused men to be his disciples. Then he asked them questions that either they couldn't answer or didn't understand, or perhaps they weren't listening to at all.

I've grown to sympathize with the disciples more and more as I've walked this world. Peter shows both depth and ignorance within the course of one conversation. Thomas doubts deeply what he can't touch. Philip needs a plan. James and John are ready to deal out some fiery punishment. The other disciples aren't even mentioned in detail, but I'm sure they had their issues.

They weren't experts. I'm not an expert, honestly. I have tons of questions and stumble more than I care to, and every once in a while, yes, I hit stride. There are things I know and can share as a gift and a help to others. From time to time I even do what Paul describes as "the good I want to do" (Romans 7:19).

It is an odd paradox, however. We look toward experts to help soothe and salve our own uncertainty and curiosity, never once thinking that those experts not only share but also *fear* the very curiosities that sit deep within us.

Why be curious when you have it all figured out and you've consulted the experts on all things "faith"?

Instead, Jesus called men who were *susceptible* to curiosity. Men who had faith, but who also worked with their hands and had real and raw personalities. They were people who had seen life as hard and jagged, unfair and unrelenting, but also simple and beautiful. They were broken in a world where life with God was presumed to be very certain.

They were truly blessed, because the great enemy of certainty is brokenness, and the great gift of brokenness is curiosity. The disciples had the feeling that being called by Jesus meant they were *fortunate*—they were blessed to just be there. They didn't understand. They didn't claim to understand. Their questions revealed they didn't understand.

They expressed what Aaron Niequist so eloquently says in his song "Here Are My Hands":

God I know / there's still just so much I just don't know.

When we know we're out of our depth, vulnerable, and unprepared, then curiosity comes quietly like a breeze. When we embrace curiosity, it becomes comfortable in our heart and mind, even if it feels awkward and demeaning when we're around others.

Sarah Lewis describes this phenomenon of how learning more leads to less certainty, also known as the Dunning-Kruger effect: "the greater our proficiency, the more clearly we recognize the possibilities of our own limitations." The closer we walk with Christ, the more we realize how far we are from his beauty and goodness, and so we ask new questions.

Growth by Questions

Jesus took the disciples and introduced them to a life of engaging the questions. For the majority of Jesus' 183 curious interactions, the disciples were seated on the front row. They asked, they heard, they watched, and they grew in wonder as Jesus opened up possibilities beyond imagination.

As they grew, they also came to recognize they had a great deal more to explore. Curiosity didn't diminish in their time with Jesus; it took flight. That's what we're invited to. We're invited to the "fellowship of those out of their depth." We're invited to walk after the Jesus who *asked* instead of told, who prompted curiosity with his every teaching and action.

Becoming curious, repenting, and rewriting our spiritual narrative through beautiful questions is also a discipline. It doesn't happen by accident. It happens when we create space for it to happen.

Our souls and our stories aren't crying out for more certainty but a move back to childlike curiosity when it comes to what God is up to in our lives. To be able to see that sometimes our certainties obscure what the good God is working in our story and in our world.

What if this curiosity helps us understand what St. John of the Cross so eloquently stated, "A soul will never grow until it is able to let go of the tight grasp it has on God"? To repent of our control of God through certainty and instead to embrace curiosity in our walk with him is what it means to accept the invitation to change our minds.

I believe that chasing questions is an act of taking Jesus' invitation to *repent*. Walking with the teachings of Jesus, and by default the questions of Jesus, with this kind of curiosity rewrites the story of God that we're living. Questions rewire us to see the kingdom of God as it is and as it can be in this moment, this time, and this place in our story.

It is an evolving story, changing with life stages and situations, so we need to continue to seek curiosity throughout our lives.

What does that look like?

That is a beautiful question.

QUESTIONS JOURNAL EXERCISE

Priming the Pump

Each exercise in this book will be geared toward opening up places for God to engage, draw out, and intensify your curiosity. In the process, I hope you'll engage in the discipline of pursuing curiosity. This will shape you to be open and available to the kind of questions that the kingdom of God brings out of every dark corner and blue sky.

It may be helpful to find a group of people to read through this book and engage in the exercises and practices together.

This chapter's exercise is a way of getting started. You can use it either as a one-time activity or use it once a day for an extended period of time.

This exercise is the practice that helped launch this book. I spent time each day for forty days writing whatever questions came to mind for that day or for that particular spot in life. Reading back over those questions, I have found rich places of prayer and pursuit that I still haven't fully engaged.

Here's how to start:

1. Find a journal, notebook, or app that makes sense for you. I recommend writing on paper as the best practice for this exercise, but it's fine if you work better in a digital medium.

2. Choose a time when you have space, it's quiet, and you can focus. It's important that you are able to let the questions flow out with the least amount of distraction.

3. Start writing. This is critical: don't edit for punctuation or spelling, don't try to clarify or reword, simply let the questions flow out of your mind as they come. There isn't a minimum or maximum number of questions; in my own practice I wrote as few as five and as many as twenty. The point is to let them come out.

4. Take a moment to read the questions you've written and prayerfully consider any themes or ideas that rise out of your writing. Consider this a practice of *quaestio divina*, "divine questioning."

5. If any one question stands out, offer it as a prayer as you end your practice.

The beauty of this Questions Journal exercise is that it can be paired with contemplative prayer, reading of Scripture, and even the practice of the Ignatian Examen. (The Examen is a prayer practice that brings us to reflect on the past day, looking for where God has been active and how we've responded to that activity. It's a perfect partner to the Questions Journal, in my opinion.)

CHAPTER TWO

growing young

Children are agents of their own learning. . . . Babies make it their own business to find out about the world.

IAN LESLIE

How do we enter
the kingdom of God?

Researchers say that children between the ages of three and five ask between three hundred and four hundred questions per day. I don't know this for sure, but I'm guessing 50 percent of those questions are one word: *why.*

When we're born, we don't come out of the womb preloaded with everything we need to know. If that were the case, we'd split atoms in preschool.

Philosopher John Locke once said we are all born with a *tabula rasa* or "blank page." That idea has been challenged, but we can see a grain of truth in it when we look at toddling toddlers and wild-eyed kindergarteners. The world is new, unique, fresh-washed and open to the mind of a child.

When we watch kids at school or at play, we see them working with a clean and wide canvas waiting for the brush that will give it unique color and beauty.

Johann Christoph Arnold says, "It is a beautiful thing to see a child thoroughly absorbed in his play; in fact it is hard to think of a purer more spiritual activity." Indeed, childhood is an object lesson in the unhindered Spirit of God throwing joy headlong into the world.

Play is a spiritual activity, primarily because it is freedom—kids have the freedom to not know, to not have an answer, and to not seek it. It is spiritual because where the Spirit of the Lord is, there is freedom (2 Corinthians 3:17).

Kids play because they typically have no mental or emotional obstacles; they have no expectations, no limits, and no boundaries. They see the world as limitless and boundless, but also as curious and mysterious.

Interestingly, when we give ourselves to disciplines like prayer, sabbath, and fasting—disciplines where God *cares* for us—we experience the care of a loving and wise Parent. Ian Leslie says that curiosity thrives in this kind of environment: "Childhood means not having to commit to a particular course of action, because adults are taking care of our survival. We can hang back, watch, question and learn what works best for us before deciding which path to take." The feeling of being safe, loved, and protected allows for exploration and frees up time to chase questions.

Kids do chase questions, asking incessantly, passionately, like desert dwellers seeking water, longing for satisfaction. They don't seem to mind being seen as naive and gullible—which they are, and I have a suspicion that they *know it*.

Kids ask questions because they know above all things that they *don't know*.

So instead of answers and knowledge, we as human beings come into this world alive with *curiosity*. We walk in freedom, we play without limits, and we ask without pride.

Loss of Childhood

Something happens to curiosity as we grow, however. Researcher Susan Engel says around four years old our curiosity begins to fade. Instead of seeing questions as dusty and interesting paths to opportunity, as we did as a child, we see questions as something that we don't have the bandwidth to handle.

As we age, questions make us vulnerable, revealing that we don't know the answer, and not knowing the answer makes us feel weak. We begin to realize how truly unguarded and fragile we are when we ask our deepest questions. When we try, after a litany of experiences and failures, to understand how God might love us and call us loved, we are mystified because *we* barely like ourselves—how can we be loved well in this state? How can we possibly approach that question?

Questions take time, and the best ones are not easily resolved in a moment, if at all. A conversation with a six-year-old will take the better part of a day. It will start and stop a thousand times, but they'll keep pushing it. We adults would rather leave well enough alone.

Questions cause us to dig with our fingers through the soil to the roots of things we already have some level of certainty about. Kids don't know yet; they haven't cemented their positions and reality. As their brain develops, they're able to handle more and more, which puts more and more on the table for debate.

So we seem to stand in this odd spot: curiosity and questions are the hard-wired, God-infused elements that make us who we are, and yet we move in our adult lives away from questions and more toward certainty because of the mess that questions create. What now?

The Root of Becoming Curious

Jesus enters into the picture and speaks to curiosity-dodging adults. I remember reading this verse and seeing things through a new lens—a new vision. "Truly I tell you, unless you change and become like little *children*, you will never enter the kingdom of heaven. Therefore, whoever takes the lowly position of this *child* is the greatest in the kingdom of heaven" (Matthew 18:3-4, emphasis added).

Children? Yes. The ones who ask the three to four hundred questions a day, the ones who are fragile and vulnerable because they realize they don't know, the ones who dig at the roots of everything that grownups take as given—is it possible that *they* are the picture Jesus has in his head when he speaks of the kingdom of God?

What does it mean to take that "lowly position"?

The hardest part of driving internationally—which I haven't done and most likely won't do—is that the lanes in some countries head in the opposite directions from the ones in the United States.

Writer Tom Smith writes about moving to the United States from his native South Africa and relearning how to drive. He had to learn how to drive on the "wrong" side of the road: "In order to become an active part of the kingdom of the United States we had to change and become like children, otherwise we would not be able to live in the States. It took some serious unlearning to *rewire* what was second nature to us. It was a form of *conversion*."

Relearning.

Rewiring.

Conversion.

He had to return to that place where he didn't know, to a blank canvas. He had to relearn something he already thought he had mastered.

It is truly "a lowly position," a position of starting over, in a sense. We begin to reexamine fundamental questions, realities, and thoughts about the world, and we do it on a regular basis. Jesus invited us to "change" (*strephō*) in the sense of *converting* or "turning toward" this childlikeness.

This kingdom, the reality of God alive and kicking in the here and now, has a kid's menu. It comes to those who want chocolate milk like it's oxygen. It comes to those who see an animal shape in every cloud, and especially to those who aren't afraid to pull the king of hearts from the house of cards that is their certainty in order to see what happens.

Jesus asks a question even as he makes this statement: *What if you became like a child? What if you stepped into this kind of attitude, the dependence and glorious poetry of knowing that you have so much more to learn, and through that you became truly great?*

Larry Crabb says it better than I can when reflecting on Jesus' invitation to become like little children:

> Nobody is more needy and has less to give than an infant. Babies never intentionally give anything of value to anyone. Sure, they can be fun to cuddle and fascinating to look at, but never because they want to be. They never look for ways to bless. They're takers through and through, not only because they're *selfish* (though they are) but because they're *helpless*. Be like that! You *are* helpless, so admit it. Learn to receive what you cannot provide for yourself.

In all honesty spiritual formation—every discipline, every retreat, every conversation, every work of mission—is a process of regressing in order to grow, to receive. The more childlike we become, the more questions we ask, the more clarity we have about this glorious kingdom of God breaking into our everyday world.

What would that look like for you, right where you are?

The whole idea of becoming a curious child is compelling to me. I'm compelled because I *am* a child. I stumble as I walk; I return curses for curses instead of learning how to bless and be a "benediction" to others (Romans 12:14).

It is, however, so easy to retreat into my carefully crafted adulthood and say, "Well, relationships are complicated." "People are strange." "You don't know our backstory." "They had it coming." "This isn't the first time." And on and on. The harder we try to remain in our certainty of adulthood, the more we end up looking like the worst version of our childhood selves: spoiled, protective, and filled with suspicion that everyone wants to take what's "ours."

At a very dark place in my life a few years ago, I was out of energy and wounded from some very difficult church experiences. I was honestly questioning whether continuing to walk in the vocation of a pastor was a good idea. Perhaps it was time to consider a new venture, a new work in the world. At that point my wife and I moved to the Chicago area and into a very different culture. We came limping, often referring to that period as a time of triage, where our wounds were being dressed and given time to heal.

During that time period, we were loved well by friends and a new church community. Each act of grace came as a surprise. We had seen flecks of grace throughout the years prior, but when you have been inhaling from the smoking barrel of conflict and chaos, it is very hard to smell the sweet strains of goodness. Our minds were being changed.

What if there is a different and healthy way to walk with Jesus?

What if there are people who see faith the way we do?

That period of our lives, a time of about two to three years, brought out some of the healthiest soul-searching questions because we were being guided along a path of shedding our preoccupations. We grasped at each new day with the grubby hands of children.

Come, Child, and Play

Part of my interest in this childlike curiosity comes from the fact that when I was seventeen I experienced the divorce of my parents. The snow fell deep that January, and as I was unloading the moving truck at my dad's new house a question slowly began to rise: *What's going to happen now?*

I remember asking him, and I'm embarrassed to think about it now, "Are you going to come back to the house for a bit?"

"No, this is it," he said.

Even at that early age, I was still trying to get my feet under me as a person in the world. What now? What does it mean to be a husband and a father? And who, if my dad maintained his distance, would script that path for me with their words and witness?

Granted, these were all curiosities painted in blacks and reds—colors of anger and frustration. Beyond that I wondered how I would handle the family dynamics that came out of this season. I would soon graduate and move on to college, leaving a ragged-edge ending to that chapter of my life.

What would happen to my sister?

What would happen to my mother?

It wasn't until many years later, when God granted me the gift of a healthy marriage relationship and some wise counselors, that I was able to look back and ask these questions in a healthy way. My dad has stayed relatively close, but we struggle with each other. I didn't handle my departure from home very well, and the connection between my growing life and my adult life became hazy and translucent. My relationships with my family are still gray, but I've tried to remain curious, asking, "What might happen now?"

The curiosity of a child helps to span the gaps of certainty with hope. And when I was uncertain in my family life I began to see spaces where Jesus invited me to ask, and to "Come, child, and play."

Jesus invites us to repent and see through the eyes of a child, to see things again for the first time. Come and revisit your stories, your wounds, and your mysteries in the light of childlike trust that "things will be okay."

I wonder if Jesus is actually saying, "Turn your head; return to that childlike curiosity that taught you about the world, that way of walking and playing and exploring. From there, you'll see the ever-brilliant kingdom of God, and you'll see it every day for the first time."

What if we embraced our story of being abused as a child—searching and asking with grubby fingers for a new story that God may be telling with that tragedy, with that wound?

What if we tore our narrative apart, the one that says God is as addicted to certainty in faith as we are, with why questions, the repetitive plea of a child?

What if we held our deepest desires in our small palms, both the simple pleas and the major asks, and extended them before curious Jesus and asked, "What about this? What do I do with this?"

Perhaps living in the kingdom of God means that our narrative—the story of how God is shaping our Spirit and soul—is a *living* document. The way you walk with it, the way you live it with health and beauty, is to learn to embrace it with curiosity.

The more we ask, the more we explore, the more we push and stretch and hold to the light, the more mystery we can stand near and yet be quieted in our soul (Psalm 131), the more penetrating our vision into the kingdom of God will become.

A Different Kind of Magic

My daughter first went to Disney World when she was five. She had already done some significant travel, but this trip was different. Mystery and magic were in her eyes because of how potent the Disney *idea* is.

The role of a parent in Disney World, at least at the onset, is to move the family from ride to ride or attraction to attraction in the most efficient way possible in order to hit all the popular rides before the lines turn into holding pens.

My wife and I had already been to Disney several times, so we had a great game plan. We knew how to move around the park and were going to make sure our daughter was able to ride all the great rides with the least amount of wait time possible. We felt the park mastery throbbing in our veins; we were going to get stuff *done*.

As we entered the park, my daughter's eyes began to dance. She saw everything in day-bright color, blasting into her field of vision and as we pounded down Main Street toward the first leg of our plan for park domination, she kept stopping.

"Look at that!"

"Oh, what's this?"

"Can we do that?"

The plan was getting derailed. We explained each epiphany without even looking up, "Yes, that's Casey's Hot Dogs. We see! Those are the rails that the parade cars run on. Yeah, the castle is pretty; we're scheduled to be there later today. Pick up the pace, kiddo!"

The park was a scheduled, contained, physical, and public situation for the adults. For the child, the curious one, it had no boundaries. It was eternal in a sense, every place with new questions and experiences. She didn't see what we saw. She saw more because she had space within her soul to receive it all as new and beautiful.

So we adults began to *repent*. We walked slower, we waited together, and we began to recapture a bit of the brilliance for ourselves. We began to think differently.

Of course Orlando isn't the complete picture of the kingdom of God, but there was something to be gained in our reintroduction to childhood. We began to see familiar things with new eyes, and in doing that we found a place of joy and a new habit of walking that breathed life into the day.

If the kingdom of God is the boundless work of a good Father for his children, why wouldn't we want to relent of our certainty? Why wouldn't we want to repent and reclaim the curiosity of a child for what might be possible if that kingdom really is "near"?

QUESTIONS JOURNAL EXERCISE

Becoming Childlike

The work of adulthood, for most of us, has become the default program setting in our brains and in our hearts. This journal exercise might be difficult because it requires that we step backward a bit, looking into places we have long closed off and left unexamined.

1. Find a quiet place and set aside a significant amount of time (15-30 minutes) to engage in this exercise.

2. In this quiet place, think about your childhood. What questions come to mind as you look at your most vivid childhood memories? What uncertainties come out of those memories? What questions would you like to have asked of the people involved in your life back then? It's important to give time for these questions to rise up; don't rush this process. Write these questions down.

3. As you look at your life today, what questions haunt you? What faith and life questions are keeping you up at night? If you have begun to keep a questions journal (see chap. 1), feel free to use some of those questions here as well.

4. Begin to look at both your questions from steps 2 and 3 and ask, How can I approach these questions as a child? What questions would arise if someone free, innocent, and curious approached the questions of my past and present life?

5. Spend some time prayerfully offering these questions to God, asking him to grant you the grace to become increasingly childlike in your everyday curiosity.

CHAPTER THREE

what do you want me to do for you?

Christians are a new creation, with new capacities.
We can now interact with the Ruler of the universe.

JAMES BRYAN SMITH

What can I do for you?

In a world where service organizations say "The customer is always right" (and even *believe* it, depending on the day), the phrase "What can I do for you?" sets the stage. It puts things in order. I am the person with the money to spend. You are my servant who will help me spend that money. My money will eventually pay your salary. So we're both happy.

My wife and I were coming back from a morning meeting and decided to stop at a local greasy spoon for breakfast. I don't know if you're aware of this, but "greasy spoon" is a romantic way of saying "nothing fancy, but still good."

You don't go there to find *actual greasy spoons.*

And yet that's *exactly* what we found.

Our feet stuck to the floor as we walked, and our hands stuck to the plastic tablecloth. The silverware was indeed greasy, having not been washed for at least a decade. And the food was what you'd expect given the other details. The blessed outcome of all this was a robust case of food poisoning and some hard-won wisdom about where we would *never* eat again.

However, even though I don't remember it, I'm sure that at some point a beautiful soul who bore the image of God came to our table and said, "What can I do for you?" The list was too long to answer that question honestly. There was too much risk in telling her the truth, so we ate, paid the bill, and quickly exited.

The relationship that comes from the beautiful question, What can I do for you? is filled with tension and risk. It creates a vulnerable situation where someone can get food poisoning and someone else may be wounded by harsh opinions or unreasonable expectations. Tension and risk, however, are familiar ground for followers of Jesus.

A Question with Skin On

To me, *risk* and *tension* are two words that completely and fully describe the beauty and adventure of the incarnation—Jesus' arrival as a human in the middle of "greasy spoon" people in order to save them from, well, *everything*: themselves, each other, and the final foe, death.

Scripture says, "The Word became flesh and blood and moved into the neighborhood" (John 1:14 *The Message*). The mysterious move of God, the *curious* move of God to send someone whole and beautiful to jump into the mess with those who are broken is a cosmic act of "What can I do for you?"

It was also a tremendous risk. Jesus, the Son of God, became vulnerable, completely, to the ebb and flow of a fragmented world. He stood in the middle of a moment to announce to anyone who was paying attention, "This is what real life looks like. This is it. This is how you stand in the midst of the mess and walk in wisdom with God."

The incarnation—Jesus coming in flesh—was *unsettling*. The things that had long been assumed about God, faith, and people were drawn into the light and turned like a diamond to catch the sun in a fresh and brilliant way. It was beautiful. It still is beautiful. For the people then and for us today it requires that we "repent" of our expectations for God and life and everything in between.

It also remains one of the more curious things about the Christian tradition. If God is a person, if the "way" or instruction is a person and not a law, then what happens now? What if he meets real people? What if he loves them? Even worse, what if he actually *likes* them? These questions *excite* me today. They're ones that, if we chase them with childlike curiosity, will shape our days with more grace than we could possibly imagine.

The problem is that people in Jesus' day already *had* a way of being in the world. They had laws, traditions, and customs that shaped and formed them to walk in wisdom with God. Why would God take a people who already had a way of being with God and send Jesus to re-envision that way of being? What kind of God changes his mind like this?

A bigger question is: *Why did God change the way his people walk in the world by sending someone whose life screamed "What can I do for you?"*

To talk about this, we have to look at three men: James, John, and Bartimaeus.

The Thunder Boys

If someone asks, "Are you going to eat that?" it is important to know where you are at that moment. If you're at home and the questioner is one of your family members, it probably makes sense. If you're in a dentist's office and have no food but are holding a magazine? That's a different story. The difference is *context*.

When it comes to Jesus' questions, context matters as well.

In the context of Mark 10, it appears that Jesus is delightfully confusing his listeners, not to frustrate them but to stoke their curiosity.

The landscape of Mark 10 is wide and colorful. Jesus first teaches two things about divorce, both of which move past the legality to the lives involved. Jesus then moves children to the front of the line headed into the kingdom, even though they were relatively worthless in that culture. Finally, Jesus suggests breaking wealth's power over a rich young man is more important than the man's faithfulness to God's commandments, which have stood since Moses. Things were tense.

On any day, those of us who follow Jesus are pressed with questions about sexuality, politics, parenting, relationships, ethics, morals, death, finances, and the creation of Earth—not necessarily in that order.

Sometimes those questions are exhausting. Sometimes we want to choose the bite-size, easy answers to make it all a little smoother. We want to avoid the tension—to avoid the risk.

Jesus, on the other hand, seemed to be running *toward* tension and risk. He risked losing his position as a dominant Jewish male by advocating for divorced women and for lowly children. He advocated selling everything and giving the proceeds to the poor, placing this action alongside the original great commandments. This of course created tension within the wealthy young man, not to mention others. Jesus looked at a rich young man and loved him, and then Jesus let him walk away. Why? Isn't the point that Jesus wants to have as many followers as possible? Why let him go?

Curious, yes?

Whatever answer we come to, it is clear that Jesus encountered moments of questioning and tension and risk as if he were not only comfortable with them but also *welcomed* them.

To top it all off, Jesus told his disciples he would be arrested, framed, and brutally executed. Then he would rise from the dead. Wow!

Which brings us to James and John.

James and John were two of Jesus' first disciples, part of the inner circle of three, along with Peter. Putting Peter's inability to control his mouth aside, James and John had their own distinction. They had a nickname—*Boanerges*, which means "sons of thunder." We'll call them the "Thunder Boys" from now on.

Here are two brash and bold men who saw power and domination as the best answer to most questions. We know these people in our own lives, the ones who use a chainsaw to solve problems that a butter knife could easily handle.

The most encouraging thing to me about the colorful, gritty folks in the Scriptures is that they reveal how gifted Jesus is at shaping diamonds out of dust. The formation of James and John, and of you and me, always begins with our ragged edges exposed. It is where the fun and adventure of formation takes flight.

When a particular village rejects Jesus, the Thunder Boys actually ask, "Would you like us to call down fire on them?" I don't know if Jesus ever utilized the face palm, but if he did this was an appropriate moment.

I have to admit that I find myself in this spot from time to time: a situation isn't moving in the right direction, and while the *best* response would be to wait and ask patient, curious questions, the drive within me is to fix it *now*, whatever it takes.

I often struggle with detaching from instant gratification, instead asking the question, *What if fixing it now is cheap and worthless compared to the pain and growth of letting Jesus walk me toward the solution?*

While watching the news of the self-described Islamic State marching across deserts, mountains, and villages, my heart is stirred to feel what James and John are feeling. Seeing the effects of abuse on children, the innocent, the poor, and the vulnerable causes my stomach to turn and my heart to long for a King who'll ride in and make everything right.

Is it possible that my desire for destruction is actually the most destructive solution? Could my desire for this ache in my gut to be excised be less about compassion and more about convenience?

James and John have been observing the entire unfolding of Mark 10, watching Jesus interact with the Pharisees, watching him with children, and watching the hopeful rich young man leave saddened. Then they hear for the third time Jesus' somber words about the end no one wanted but seemed inevitable—Jesus repeating it three times made it that way.

In that moment the Thunder Boys become curious. If Jesus is who we think he is, the powerful Messiah come to rule the world, then we should be a part of it somehow. If someone's exerting power, we want in on that.

No B-List Requests

I remember every Christmas season as a kid waiting for the giant Sears Christmas catalog. It came in at just under one thousand pages and weighed about as much as a Toyota. It contained anything and everything you could want for Christmas. The Internet has robbed us of those glory days.

I would find a quiet place and flip through the glossy pages of action figures, sports equipment, bikes, scooters, skateboards, and video games until I had seen everything at least twice. Then I would pull out a pencil and a piece of paper and start writing. It was the list of all lists.

I would typically end up with one full page, front and back, of Christmas requests. At my house we still did the Santa thing, so I made the list with the expectation that an all-powerful, quasi-divine being could handle pretty much everything on that list. I didn't hold back—this was *Santa*.

I can't blame James and John—they are often seen in this passage as selfish and greedy for power, but they're simply acting on what they believe. If Jesus is who we think he is, he can do anything. We want to be a part of that. It is a curious moment, but it challenges us to think—if we had that opportunity, that moment to ask, why wouldn't we bring our biggest and our boldest requests to Jesus?

They come to Jesus and say, "Teacher, we want you to do for us whatever we ask" (Mark 10:35).

Jesus says, "What do you want me to do for you?" (Mark 10:36).

Now that is an incredibly curious question.

Jesus' response is filled with beauty, but also with tension and risk for James and John. Jesus actually acknowledged and encouraged what they were about to say next. He didn't shut them down or teach them a lesson, shaking his head in exasperation. He welcomed the question. He was teaching them to be curious.

In this curiosity lesson we see a glimpse of the gratuitous God that Jesus knew and loved. We see the God who gives with glee, totally unrestrained. John Flavel says, "He is bread to the hungry, water to the thirsty, a garment to the naked, healing to the wounded; and whatever a soul can desire is found in Him."

James and John step into the moment and boldly request, "Let one of us sit at your right and the other at your left in your glory" (Mark 10:37).

In other words, they wanted to be co-vice presidents with Jesus. Again, this makes sense if we think about James and John deep at their core. Jesus wasn't surprised by their question. He knew them well—what they were hoping and longing for by approaching him. Yet he invited the request and opened the door wide saying, "What do you want me to do for you?" But how would he respond to what seems to be an out of bounds, over the top, beyond their pay grade kind of request?

Cue the lightning bolts, we might think. *Unauthorized question.*

There are tense moments early on in any relationship—a friendship, a dating relationship, even a working relationship—where we hold off on asking for anything that goes over and above normal human interaction. We don't typically ask people to borrow their car or a huge sum of cash within the first few days of knowing them. We wait, we earn trust and learn to trust, and we grow in our friendship.

The reason Jesus' questions are so important to our formation is that they welcome us into a new way of knowing him. They shape us by inviting us to a bigger conversation, a deeper level of trust, and a new way of seeing reality. James and John had traveled, eaten, and worked alongside Jesus. They had a relationship where they could ask. However, they were about to have their reality reordered, and with them we learn a huge lesson about curiously engaging with Jesus.

You Don't Always Know

Jesus responds to James and John: "You don't know what you are asking. . . . Can you drink the cup I drink or be baptized with the baptism I am baptized with?" (Mark 10:38). I wonder if James and John at this point began to regret asking the question.

In 2006, my mother-in-law became incredibly sick. After testing and struggle it was determined that her liver was failing and she would need a transplant. The curious thing about the whole situation was that we prayed constantly for her to get better—for the symptoms to fade, for God to heal her miraculously. It was an incredibly difficult season for all of us, but in the end she received a new liver and has gone right on living.

As we reflected on that season, we realized that our prayers *couldn't* have been answered early on. Receiving the liver transplant was based on her condition getting *worse*, and so healing those early symptoms would have ultimately killed her. I imagine Jesus in that moment saying, "I can see what you can't see. Ask me and trust me, definitely, but also trust me for what actually happens."

When Jesus asked James and John about the "cup" and the "baptism" I imagine they began to look downward. James and John would have known *cup* and *baptism* to be metaphors for suffering and even death. Jesus' question drew them back to reality, brought their request for power and position into a different light, and humbled them immensely.

"You don't know what you're asking." That's a moment when we *learn* something. Curiosity may invite us into risk and tension, but it can also readjust the way we see reality. That's what it means to be a "learner"—a disciple—of Jesus.

It is easy to see this moment as one to fear, the feeling of being exposed by Jesus. To hear "you don't know what you're asking" sounds like *failure* to us. It sounds like Jesus is always the smart one (which he is) and we are always incompetent. But the real sweetness of this interaction is in the *teaching* that comes through Jesus' words. We learn the heart, the meat even, of what we're asking when we place it in front of Jesus.

To be invited into this curious discussion, to hear Jesus say, "What do you want me to do for you?" is to throw back the curtain on the reality of following Jesus in the real and gritty world. Humility, not power, is the key. His way is going to be one of struggle, even of death, because the world has seen enough of domination and force. James and John say, "Yes, we can drink that cup and be baptized with your baptism. We're ready."

For the Thunder Boys, as for us, there is still more to learn.

Jesus said, "You will drink the cup I drink and be baptized with the baptism I am baptized with, but to sit at my right or left is not for me to grant. These places belong to those for whom they have been prepared" (Mark 10:39-40).

In other words, you are going to walk into the tension with me and because of me. You are going to risk greatly and find your way into struggle and death because of me. It isn't going to be a power thing, because that isn't for you to carry out. The way you walk in the world will be the way of humility, just like me.

So should they have asked Jesus for a promotion? That's the key question. Would they have been better off never going to Jesus and making what seems to be an outrageous demand? I believe this discussion was critical for James, John, and even the rest of the disciples, who were furious that the Thunder Boys would even ask the question.

With every question from Jesus, whether he's asking in response to someone else or initiating the conversation himself, we see reality repainted and refocused. James and John's request and the conversation that came out of it helps us see that the world can be reimagined if we are willing to be humbled.

Jesus is often welcoming his disciples—James and John in this case, but you and me as well—into the risk and tension of reimagining the world in the way he sees it. They had been waiting for a warlike Messiah who would blow away their enemies, but Jesus said, "Whoever wants to become great among you must be your servant, and whoever wants to be first must be slave of all. For even the Son of Man did not come to be served, but to serve, and to give his life as a ransom for many" (Mark 10:44-45).

We have to be humbled if we're going to seek other ways. The way forward isn't power. The way we all have come to understand change isn't by force, but by submission in leadership. Sacrifice. In the words of Henri Nouwen, it is all about "downward mobility."

We risk stepping onto unsure ground, exploring new places intellectually and emotionally to find where God is working and guiding us to go.

We enter the tension of Jesus saying, "Yes, but" to some of our curious requests. It may be hard, but this "yes, but" is a gift. A blessing.

And it all begins with a question, "What do you want me to do for you?"

Then There's Bartimaeus

If I ask my wife, "What can I do to help you?" a set of expectations comes with her response. Typically, helping her has an impact on me—I get to eat what we're preparing for dinner; I get to enjoy a clean house or clean laundry; I get to share in the joy of partnering as parents.

However, if I ask a stranger, say someone struggling with their bags on a windy Chicago street, there are different expectations. It is most likely a one-time thing. Generally speaking, reaching out to those closest to us is easier and more natural than extending ourselves to a stranger.

James and John are in the inner circle of the disciples. They have privileged access to Jesus, and it makes sense that they would take advantage of their situation and engage Jesus on the question of power and place.

But a blind man? A stranger? A beggar along the road?

Jesus and his disciples come to Jericho, a bustling Jewish city expecting Jesus and which had no doubt heard about his fame. Crowds had gathered, shouting and cheering, awaiting the famous rabbi who occasionally did miraculous things.

As they approached, a blind man named Bartimaeus began to shout from the side of the road, "Son of David, have mercy on me!" (Mark 10:47).

Two things in this scene help to make sense of what we read: first, the name Bartimaeus should actually read "Bar-Timaeus," which means "son of Timaeus." His name, his identity, was based on who his father was. He had no identity of his own. Younger siblings get this—"Oh you're so-and-so's little sister (or brother)." They have no identity.

Second, Bartimaeus was blind and a beggar, therefore he was considered worthless in society. Daily, he would sit by the major roadways, spread out his cloak in front of him, and wait for donations. Much like a street performer who puts out his guitar case and hopes for donations, Bartimaeus begged to survive.

Charity. He had no other choice.

So when Bartimaeus, this outsider, this helpless man, began shouting to Jesus, the crowd attempted to shut him down.

Who do you think you are?

Why would he even look in your direction?

But the Jesus walking the road to Jericho had an ear for those at the margins, those who had no identity, those whose world had fallen apart. Jesus stops and says, "Call him" (Mark 10:49).

Jesus once again invites someone, makes a way for this person to step into his presence bringing their whole soul with them, tatters and all. Everyone around saw this as a moment of tremendous risk. *What would this blind man do?* "Those people" can't be trusted, you know.

In walking with Jesus, being shaped to be like him, we find ourselves in the position of Bartimaeus far more often than that of the Thunder Boys. We feel weak and blind, and we stumble toward God with every ounce of our energy. It's good to hear Jesus welcome Bartimaeus, to know that those who feel powerless are welcomed into Jesus' loving presence.

Bartimaeus jumps to his feet and *casts his cloak aside* on the way to Jesus (Mark 10:50). It seems like a small action, a small detail, but when Bartimaeus tosses his cloak he throws to the wind any donations he received that day. Remember, the cloak was his paper cup or guitar case; it was his only sure thing.

Bartimaeus takes a huge risk and has an opportunity to speak with the one who can radically alter his life, Jesus, the Son of David. It's a moment filled with possibility and promise. Perhaps this is the moment he will become something more than just the son of Timaeus.

What happens next is incredible, a moment of pure curiosity.

Jesus says to Bartimaeus, "What do you want me to do for you?" (Mark 10:51). It's the same question Jesus posed to the Thunder Boys. I can imagine James and John listening to this interaction with their mouths hanging open. *He got the same invitation we did! How is that possible?*

It is interesting to think about Jesus' question from the disciples' point of view. When Jesus says to a *blind man,* "What do you want me to do for you?" I imagine Peter nudging Jesus and saying, "I think the blindness is a good place to start. Then again, that's just me."

Jesus doesn't take the obvious route. He doesn't immediately address what appears to everyone to be the greatest issue. He invites Bartimaeus to be a part of the discussion. He invites the nameless blind man at the margins to request whatever he wants of Jesus. Ask for what you desire, and we'll go from there.

Bartimaeus replies, "Rabbi, I want to see."

"'Go,' Jesus said. 'Your faith has healed you.' Immediately he received his sight and followed Jesus along the road" (Mark 10:51-52).

It may have been Bartimaeus's faith, but Jesus' *question* made all the difference. It was Jesus' welcome, his invitation, and his attention to one who didn't merit attention that created a miraculous moment on an ordinary day in Jericho.

When I teach sessions on prayer, a question comes up consistently: "Is it okay to ask for things for ourselves?"

For whatever reason, we have a concept that God is not concerned with what we need, want, or desire. We can ask for things for other people, we can ask to be forgiven, and we can give words of worship, but when it comes to requests for ourselves, God has no place for that kind of thing.

But then there's Jesus, standing patiently, saying, "What do you want me to do for you?"

If we are going to walk a new way in the world, being shaped at the deepest parts of our torn and misguided hearts, we're going to have to engage Jesus in this question. We need to come to terms with a God who is actually interested in what we long for and desire.

This curious question of Jesus' gives us an opportunity to redeem desire, even if only to learn a new way of seeing things through the lens of God's kingdom. Regarding desire, Jen Pollock Michel says, "The Gospel of Jesus Christ meets our holy hesitations about desire, without eliminating the tension or minimizing the dangers, yet suggesting it can be reformed."

Sometimes we come frustrated, overwhelmed, and powerless in the face of our circumstances. James, John, and Bartimaeus encountered Jesus in a moment when they were searching for a change, for a solution.

To blindness.

To injustice.

To oppression.

They felt the frustration of the psalmist:

> How long must I bear pain in my soul,
>   and have sorrow in my heart all day long?
> How long shall my enemy be exalted over me?
>   (Psalm 13:2 NRSV)

Have you ever felt this kind of frustration? What do you want him to do for you?

Jesus' response was a way of shaping the men's spirits—their wills, drives, and desires—so they would walk differently as a result of responding to his question. This is why curiosity is such a critical discipline: without engaging with Jesus' questions, these men (and those of us walking with Jesus today) would have missed a transformational moment of epic proportions.

Finding Joy in the Ordinary

As I walked through the Mathare Valley slums in northeastern Nairobi, Kenya, my heart was torn. I watched children playing beside rivers of sewage; they played in it as human waste floated by. With looks of joy and mischief, they exposed themselves to bacteria that would shut down public buildings in the United States.

The effects of global poverty are complicated, for sure. Statistics and reports are helpful, but when you're standing face to face with a child, with the stinging smell of humanity pounding your nostrils, righteous anger reduces the options quickly, and the thought that comes to mind is, *Someone needs to do something about this. Now!*

Yet there is joy in the faces of these children, in the pride of the single mother of four children who showed me her corrugated tin shack with the single light bulb. Despite all circumstances there is joy. It isn't easy to solve the problem of global poverty, but it starts with people like you and me standing in the middle of the tension—taking the risk of having our hearts broken permanently—and hearing Jesus say, "What do you want me to do for you, right here and now?"

Sometimes we come blind, pushed to the margins because of things, whether within or outside our control, that make us outcasts. We're known as addicts or adulterers or ex-cons. We sit by the road waiting for something to change and someone who might redeem our situation.

Instead Jesus comes and asks, "What do you want me to do for you, right now, where you are?" Is it really that simple?

When it came to Bartimaeus, everything changed. He couldn't beg for a living anymore, being that he was no longer blind, and so he would have to get a job like everyone else.

Jesus rescued Bartimaeus and inserted him into a very normal, regular life. We imagine the "What do you want me to do for you?" question turning into a miraculous festival of fireworks, but what if instead we're rescued to a life of simple meals, difficult circumstances, and good, hard, sweaty work?

The most amazing thing about any sort of work of God—miraculous healings, health restoration, and so on—is that afterward you'll still need bread and milk. Bills will need to be paid. Hard conversations will need to happen. We have experienced a miraculous happening that shapes a very normal story.

If in this moment Jesus were to ask you, "What do you want me to do for you?" how would you respond?

If he asks the question, are you ready to risk the "cup" and the "baptism"? What if some pride has to die in the process? What if you have to throw your cloak to the wind and leave certainty behind to engage in a curious classroom with the ever-present brilliance of Jesus?

What if the answer to your request isn't a dynamic celebrity-caliber life but instead a beautiful new normal that roots you in the everyday world in a different way?

If so, then what do you want him to do for you?

QUESTIONS JOURNAL EXERCISE

Come Asking

Jesus posed a significant question to James, John, and Bartimaeus: *What do you want me to do for you?*

I imagine these three men had no clue what was coming. They were taking a risk, stepping out, and testing the waters with the unpredictable and brilliant Jesus. Regardless of their intentions, all three received more than they were expecting.

What are you expecting today? What are you willing to risk in order to hear that question, *What do you want me to do for you?*

In this questions journal exercise, we want to get into a place where we can pursue Jesus' question *curiously*—expressing what the deepest parts of our soul want, but also understanding that we may learn about our *desires* and get a different view of reality in the meantime.

The following are some suggestions for creating a habit of engaging curiously with Jesus, along with James, John, and Bartimaeus. This exercise can be repeated multiple times, reflecting at different stages and seasons of life on Jesus' question.

1. Start by finding a quiet place to write. Make sure that you have some dedicated time in which you won't be interrupted.

2. List all of your responses to Jesus' question, "What do you want me to do for you?" Don't edit your words; let them flow as they come. Typically your first thoughts reflect the stuff that is most important to you.

3. Imagine yourself sitting at a table with Jesus when he asks, "What do you want me to do for you?" Which of your responses in suggestion 2 will you offer him?

4. Spend some time listening. Clear your mind and focus on what Jesus says to your response. Write down anything significant that comes from this practice.

As with any of the questions journal practices, make sure to come back to what you write here and reflect on it. Make notes on what has changed over time since you spent time with Jesus engaging with this question.

CHAPTER FOUR

a question of identity

Identity is never simply a creation. It is always
a discovery. True identity is always a gift of God.

DAVID BENNER

Who do you think you are?

The office was cold and clinical, painted in that kind of stark white used in hospitals and counselors' offices—places where pain typically *increases* before it is relieved.

I waited. I happened to be in the office as part of a job interview process. The person I was waiting to see was a specialist in reading personality tests who would reflect on my unique personality before recommending that the company hire me, or not.

I hoped I had passed.

When the specialist came in, the mood immediately shifted. I felt adversity in the air. The posture, greeting, and initial questions were formal and had a razor-sharp edge to them. I'm an extrovert, so I'm used to meeting new people, getting through the initial weirdness, and leveling out to where I feel comfortable, so I wasn't really worried. But I never got comfortable.

The interview was a constant debate, each positive answer I gave was countered with "Why do you believe that?" or "What makes you think that's true?" They weren't gentle or inquisitive questions but aggressive and almost condescending.

Things were not going according to my expectations.

Finally, the interviewer asked what I planned on doing if I got the job. I answered as best I could, trying to remain calm but confident. I knew this person would report back to the interview committee, so I couldn't blow it. His response was like a lightning strike right at my feet: "Who do you think you are?"

I didn't know how to respond. I stuttered and stumbled over my words as I made my way through the rest of the interview, and then we were done. As I drove the two hours home I thought, *I blew it. That was awful. What happened there?*

My wife, who works in human resources, looked blankly at me as I described the horrors of my day and then said, "You just had a stress interview."

Who Do You Think You Are?

The question "Who do you think you are?" has stuck with me since then, because I have to answer that question on a daily—if not hourly—basis. I believe we all do. When we are put to the test by our job (which is what the stress interview was designed to measure), we are pressed to prove who we are and why we matter.

When our marriages grow rocky and awkward, we deal with it from the place of who we really believe we are.

When our relationships with friends grow lopsided, codependent, and even abusive, we have to wrap our arms around who we believe we are.

When we have to muster the confidence to go on another date, in search of the person who will be our companion on the journey, we clothe ourselves with the question "Who do you think you are?"

Even simple social-media interactions can become a shouting match, the virtual crowd saying, "Prove yourself! Show us your vacation pictures and prove that you are someone!"

"Who do you think you are" is repeated over and over as part of our daily "stress interview."

Watching the lives of people through counseling, teaching, and spiritual direction, I've come to realize that the razor-sharp threads of bad decisions and ill-advised words are often attached to that one solitary question, "Who do you think you are?"

Jesus himself addresses this very topic.

Strange Place for a Chat

It has been quite a walk. Jesus and the disciples, breathless and thirsty, come to rest near a bustling city. They see the lights burning from distant oil lamps, the sounds of trade and shouting roll toward them in waves.

The city is Caesarea Philippi. The town used to be called Paneas, named after the ancient Greek god Pan. Darkness threatens to overcome us when we read that early Pan followers were formed by habits of child sacrifice and sexual acts with goats as part of their worship. The followers of Pan worshiped in Caesarea Philippi because they believed Pan himself lived in a cave in that region.

The name Caesarea Philippi comes from two names, actually. *Philippi* is from Philip the tetrarch, a political figure who named the region after himself. Philip, it appears, was a big fan of Philip. *Caesarea* comes from Roman emperor Caesar Augustus. This emperor was ruthless and confident. He believed, in fact, that he was a god.

So Jesus and his disciples enter into a region that is known for an old, dark religion and is named for two self-centered and corrupt rulers who long to be seen as the highest and greatest—gods, even. In this place it is easy to become disoriented and distracted. Jesus' voice cracks through the tension:

"Who do people say the Son of Man is?" (Matthew 16:13).

The question, at least as we read it in Matthew, comes out of nowhere. The disciples are still wiping the dust from their legs and faces, preparing to rest beside a fire trying to come to life. As they reach the halfway point between standing and sitting, Jesus asks this question.

Who do people say the Son of Man is?

The "Son of Man" was a concept everyone around the fire would have recognized. The Son of Man was a hero of sorts, a legend. He was the one God would anoint. God would commission this person to be king over Israel and bring about the just, wondrous, and beautiful rule of God over the world.

Enemies would be scattered.

Oppression would cease.

Freedom would come for slaves and those in deep debt.

As they walked together, no doubt, the disciples looked at this person—this magnificent Jesus—through eyes squinting against the sun and wondered, *Is that him? The Son of Man? I think he might be.*

Now Jesus is asking what other people think about this Son of Man character. Is Jesus actually curious and interested in what people have to say? Jesus never seemed to be the type to welcome the tabloid rumors, but the table is now set for the disciples to share what they've heard.

It seems like a rich moment to help the disciples rediscover that childlike curiosity. He welcomes them to think through what they've heard, all the while using their "what's the point of this" perspective to help them know that public opinion is just part of life. People will always think things about you.

The disciples give a number of quality answers, *flattering answers*, at least to a Jewish person.

John the Baptist, back from the dead.

Elijah, back from the dead.

Jeremiah or one of the prophets, also, back from the dead.

Not only did people think Jesus was a legendary figure, they also apparently thought he was a long-dead hero brought back to life. Not bad.

The problem is that each of these people, and actually the whole belief system that colored the idea of the Son of Man, came with certain *expectations*. If you're Elijah, back from the dead, then these are the things you have to do.

Fulfill these expectations, and we'll believe in you.

Let us down, and we'll pull the rug right out from under you.

Echoes of this conversation between Jesus and the disciples reverberate within us today.

In the search for our own identity we all carry the markers and expectations of other people, markers that have made their way into us.

Scars.

Accolades.

Trophies.

Failures.

All of these mile markers in our journey have named us, have called us something, and we must choose what we do with that.

The great gift of spiritual formation, being shaped into a person who at the very depths of their being longs to live as Jesus would, is that it can engage our marks, our identity. The discipline of curiosity allows us to not only see ourselves for who we really are but also to repent of believing we will never be anything more than that.

Jesus knew there was no better way for him to reach tenderly but incisively into the disciples' minds and turn their ideas, thoughts, and understandings upside down. He knew how to help them repent in the true sense of the word—to change their minds about what was happening around them and in them as they sat in the fading light of Caesarea Philippi.

Perhaps that's where we find ourselves today. We've been off-balance, out of our element, forced to see our enemies succeed while we are stuck or in decline.

Perhaps we're in that country, so far from knowing who we are or where we're headed, and now we're outside the range of familiar voices to help us recapture the perspective we need.

In a disoriented place like this, in a "stress interview," we not only wonder why our feet have wandered this path but begin to wonder who we are, who we have become, and what has brought us to this place. Maybe it feels like a place where God *shouldn't* be found. We acutely feel our lack, our insufficiency to belong to such a good and beautiful God.

It seems as if Jesus' bringing the disciples to the edge of this misguided city is a way of engaging their curiosity about Jesus' *own* character:

Why would Jesus even bother to be in such a place—Caesarea Philippi?

Isn't this the kind of place that a person of high moral standards, an observant Jewish man such as Jesus, would want to avoid at all costs?

Not to mention the fact that it was a solid two-day journey from the village of Magadan, where the disciples had likely reconnected with Jesus. It seems awkward and ill-fitting. The disciples were used to Jesus presenting challenging situations and scenarios, but they probably had some questions:

Why are we far from home, around people of suspicious and threatening motives?

Why do we have to witness two power-hungry rulers praised and put on display for everyone to see?

What's the point of being off-balance and out of our element like this?

We come to our own Caesarea Philippi when the chapters of our story have ripped our identity from our hands, torn like a beloved toy from the hands of a child and shredded in front of us over and over again. We come to our own Caesarea Philippi when we allow others to name us—those around us who, to be sure, are only speaking out of their own destructive "names."

With all of the challenge of being off-balance, out of our element, and weary from the journey, what might we hear from Jesus in this place? Our guard is down and our hearts are aching: what word could be the drop of water that falls in this desert place?

A Place Card at the Table

The faux-gold plates make an off-pitch clinking sound as they pass down the row. Every week our community shares in Communion; some know it as Eucharist or the Lord's Supper. We take small pieces of crispy cracker bread and thimbles full of juice as a sign of the great mystery we're all joined in.

I cannot recall or count how many times I have heard people say, "I didn't take Communion this week. I just didn't feel worthy." For whatever reason, their souls pushed back from the table.

Jesus welcomes, he calls, and he invites. He says, "Drink and eat, know that you're a part of me and I'm a part of you." Picture Jesus in this invitation for a moment: a gentle smile, anticipation in his eyes. He is patiently waiting and welcoming each one of us.

And yet something in my friends causes them to push away. They don't deserve it. They need to get their acts together or check off more boxes and then they can come to the table.

Meanwhile, at their seat is a place card. Eloquently scripted by the fingers that shaped the heavens, it says their name. Their *real* name, not the one they've been given or that they've given themselves based on a litany of failures and perceived unforgiveable acts. Their real, God-engraved name.

In our life on this path there is no practice that speaks more deeply about who we really are than the breaking of bread and the spilling of blood. Filling stomachs and sustaining blood vessels and tissues tells the truth in bold print: you are named by One who died for that name and for your sake.

These elements are one of the few remaining moments of mystery that we are invited to step into, to savor, and it is completely bewildering.

Curiosity and the Lord's Supper seem to make sense together—one of the world's greatest mysteries of love brought into such simple images and elements.

Every time we eat and drink, our gaze shifts. We are asked to believe we are worth the life of Jesus, we are asked to believe those around us are as well, and we enter into this new identity wondering what it might possibly mean to our comings and goings in everyday life.

So what if we engaged this practice in our own community, in our own soul, saying, "Here are the bread and wine. Who do they say that I am?"

A New Name

The air begins to stir, the night is settling, and the cool breezes are flowing in and around the tired bodies of the disciples. They wet their lips, fresh from sharing the news of what everyone else thought about the Son of Man.

Jesus hasn't said anything for a while, they think. *What does that mean?*

Do they expect Jesus to be surprised? Do they expect him to become introspective, thinking, *That's a lot to live up to. How many times have I failed to meet those expectations? Maybe I'm not who everyone thinks?*

The last question, "Maybe I'm not who everyone thinks I am?" is a stream of living water.

The likely answer to that question is "No, you're not," and that's the most liberating gift our spirits can bear. We, the disciples, and every human crawling God's beautiful earth need to be *renamed*—daily, weekly, even hour to hour.

Jesus knew who he was, deep down. He had been given his identity long before, hearing his father say, "This is my Son, whom I love; with him I am well pleased" (Matthew 3:17).

Before he did anything—before Jesus said a word or healed a wound, before he ever blessed a loaf of bread or taught from the Scriptures—he was called "beloved" and a source of God's pleasure.

What does that mean for us?

One of the most glorious things about Jesus is that he moves past the external circumstances of a person's life, reaching deeply, like a heart surgeon, into the ventricles of their heart.

At one point Jesus was reclining at a table, eating dinner in the house of a very prominent person. In other words, the person who invited Jesus had a high profile and a rich reputation in the community.

Dinners in those days, especially with celebrity guests like Jesus, were typically open-air settings where the important guests were eating at the table, but others could easily walk by and observe the meal. In the middle of the dinner a woman overcome with her identity, her failure, and her past came in and began weeping at Jesus' feet.

She wept *on* his feet.

She kissed his feet.

Then she wiped the salt-stinging tears off of his feet, wiping them away with her own hair.

It's important to know that Jesus would have been lying on his side with his feet stretched out behind him. To touch someone's feet was intimate and sexually suggestive, so this moment was filled with tension. This was a scandal waiting to happen.

Being at that desperate, broken place where you crawl to the feet of Jesus and weep out all the bile and backstabbing, slices and slights, foolishness and failure means you are at the verge of a new and wonderful awakening.

We use phrases like "hitting bottom" or having "a moment of clarity" when this full stop comes as a result of our own failures. Clearly, failure is part of this woman's story, but as we hear more about the meal and the reaction to her, an identity crisis emerges.

The host, the prominent man with the reputation, said, "If this man [Jesus] were a prophet, he would know who is touching him and what kind of woman she is—that she is a sinner" (Luke 7:39). He expected Jesus to run away from contaminated, tainted, broken people like this woman. He would have known, God would have informed Jesus, about her past.

He named the woman *sinner*. She was her faults and failings. Jesus should have known her "name."

Jesus, however, stood quiet and firm on his identity as beloved of God—the one who gave God pleasure—and then he gave the woman a fresh and new name. She is not who everyone thinks she is.

She is one who knows how to love, and she has loved me well. She has loved me in a way that God would and in a way that you, my host, didn't even attempt. She is no longer the sum total of her ragged journey (Luke 7:44-47, my paraphrase).

She is well.

She is welcomed.

She is beloved.

She is one in whom God is well pleased.

The man of reputation only saw her *action* and *reputation*, and identified her by these. Jesus knew her identity and set her free to *act* differently. With one breath, he renamed her formally in the sight of everyone:

Then Jesus said to her, "Your sins are forgiven" (Luke 7:48).

Who Named You?

My parents were children of the 1960s and 1970s. One day in the midst of my teenage years I asked how they chose my name.

"We're not sure," they said. "We had some other names picked out, and if you had been a girl we would have named you Rhiannon."

Curious. Where did that come from?

The name Rhiannon came to my parents through a song on Fleetwood Mac's self-titled and highly successful album *Fleetwood Mac*. If you dig a little deeper, however, you find that Rhiannon was a powerful figure in early Celtic and Welsh mythology, perhaps even thought of as a goddess. She was typically associated with horses, and rode stoically around the Welsh countryside, a strong and vibrant woman doing whatever she pleased.

I imagine my parents were glad they didn't have to deal with a teenage Rhiannon.

When we realize our name and what it means, we also know how fragile names and naming can be. Granted, I wasn't born a girl, but the other name they had for a boy was Byron. Would I have been a different person had they named me Byron and not Casey? All of it came down to this for my parents:

"We just liked the name Casey better."

I love my parents, and I love my name, but there is a deep reality in this naming process. The people around us are fickle, just like the voices swirling around the grieving woman who wept on Jesus' feet.

She is Sinner.

She is Unclean.

She is Unworthy.

Sometimes a name is stamped onto our foreheads without understanding what that name will do to us.

Often those who name us are voices that don't know us deeply, at our core. They are people who don't see us as we are, a walking *poem* of God (Ephesians 2:10; "handiwork" in Greek is *poema*, the same word for poem). Perhaps they *should* know us: they are family or a spouse or a friend, but they themselves have been shaped by a broken name and are simply passing on what they have learned.

We also need to be aware of the danger of giving others the *right* to name our identity. Parker Palmer observes,

We need to see how often we conspire in our own deformation: for every external power bent on twisting us out of shape, there is a potential collaborator within us. When our impulse to tell the truth is thwarted by threats of punishment, it is because we value security over being truthful. When our impulse to side with the weak is thwarted by threats of lost social standing, it is because we value popularity over being a pariah.

We may actually admire the ones who name us, tilting our heads toward them when they sing our praise and covering our eyes with shame when they criticize us. We need them too much to offend them, to have them remove their "blessing," which is actually a curse.

Either way, the person we give the right to name our identity also gets the right to form our spirits. Our will, our motivation, our priorities, goals, hopes, and dreams will all be pressed into their mold and held up to their standards. Then we are on the chase. We will hardly know ourselves or where we are going. We will be lost.

So who named you?

What would our lives look like if each day we took on the name Forgiven or Welcomed at the Table of God?

Guilt by Association

"But what about you? . . . Who do you say I am?" (Matthew 16:15).

Jesus breaks the silence. The disciples' eyes have wandered in wonder toward the city and its sounds. Jesus becomes personal, intimate. He borrows on the trust they had built, traveling and living in each other's presence.

"I want to know what *you* think."

With all the expectations of others swept away, perhaps even those of his disciples, this question is pure and good. How the people who really know you—as far as you've let them in and given them time to learn your way of being in the world—think of you is so much more powerful.

Jesus inspires and invokes their childlike curiosity here, because from what they had seen of Jesus' life and actions there was a great deal they could have said in reply.

Miracle worker.

Friend of the poor.

Friend of sinners.

Instigator.

Revolutionary.

Friend.

The disciples had seen all of this and more, and here was a moment when Jesus opened the door and asked them to weave everything together. Bringing up the contents of their hearts, minds, and experience, they were drawn to the moment.

But why?

Again, Jesus didn't need confirmation of who he was. He knew he was the beloved One, the source of God's great pleasure. This question was about something other than Jesus' need to be named. It was also about something more than a divine pop quiz for his ragtag band of followers.

The souls of disciples—both the twelve around the fire at Caesarea Philippi and those of us who travel with Jesus today—are shaped, sustained, and known in relationship to Jesus. We are *with* him. We are becoming like the One with whom we walk.

We die with him and live again (Romans 6).

We have died. We no longer live, and Christ lives within us (Galatians 2).

I believe we need to gently and curiously explore Jesus' question "Who do you say that I am?" because our conclusion about Jesus becomes true of us.

If I say he is the one who brings the world back into order, then I'm saying that I have a part in that work. What does that look like in my job, my family, and my inner world?

If I say he is the one who "walks truth"—that is, he isn't a set of statements to be memorized and checked off—then I am walking the truth behind him and with him. What does that look like in my story today?

If I believe he is the beloved, the object of God's pleasure, does that mean I am a beloved as well—that God takes pleasure in me, as mysterious and improbable as that is?

Above all, what needs to shift within me, at the core of who I am, in order to allow those beliefs to have full reign in my life? What practices, habits, attitudes, and realities are now possible because he is who he is, and therefore I can be the same?

The conversation outside the gates of Caesarea Philippi is not a theology lesson or about getting the doctrines about Jesus correct. No, it's a lesson in identity through *identification*. When our identity is rooted, expanded, and given by Jesus, then we no longer need the many elements of being wrongly named in order to survive.

Robert Mulholland says, "Identity and value are found in a vital and living relationship with Christ as Lord. This relationship liberates Christians from dependence upon their little systems of order and fragile structures of control." The exhaustion of doing image management, maintaining the respect and approval of others, and other measures of managing our world can be released to fly like a hot air balloon. They will not return.

In Jesus we can trust our identity enough to say yes when we mean yes and no when we mean no. In Jesus we can enter solitude and silence, away from the eyes and suggestions of others, and truly enjoy the presence of the God who calls us beloved.

Under the torrent of insults, threats, and character assassinations we can trust that we are held and hidden, and the force of others cannot remove our identity.

Invited to the Family

Jesus had been named by God as beloved long before he asked his
disciples, "Who do people say the Son of Man is?" Before he ever
broke a sabbath "rule," sat with a prostitute, or ate without washing
his hands, Jesus knew the depths of who he was.

His name would always be "beloved Son."

Without that, the rest of the grand Jesus narrative would never have
been written. Too many expectations from other people would have
paralyzed the good story that God intended to write through him. It
is the same with us.

The great call of our identity in Jesus is that we are "who we are"
before we're asked to do a thing. We are invited to obey commands to
love and justice, but not until we've been named as those God shows
love and gives justice to.

What if this is the way the world is changed? What if the things
we mourn, we protest, we lay awake at night thinking about are all
hanging where our identity ends up? Does that feel like too much
pressure? If God loves us deeply and finds pleasure in us, can that
sustain us as we face our own gritty circumstances and consequences?

As Parker Palmer says, "I cannot give what I do not possess, so I
need to know what gifts have grown up within me that are now ready
to be harvested and shared. . . . Like the fruit of a tree, they will
replenish themselves in due season."

What would it look like to so deeply find our identity in Jesus that
we were renewed from the inside out simply by knowing what is
growing within us? What are the fruits that come when I live into,
and out of, this new identity?

What story could God be writing through us, right now, if we
weren't so consumed by the stories others have grafted deep into our
souls but instead were renewed by the identity Jesus gives?

Curious, isn't it?

The Name Changer

The closing scene of the Caesarea Philippi conversation is quite interesting. Peter responds to Jesus' question saying, "You are the Messiah, the Son of the living God" (Matthew 16:16). In other words: *Jesus, this is who you are and so this is who I am. I'm with you.*

Jesus' response is compassionate and transformational. He blesses Simon and says, "I tell you that you are Peter, and on this rock I will build my church, and the gates of Hades will not overcome it" (Matthew 16:17-18).

Jesus *renames* Peter. The name Peter literally means "rock," but Jesus is giving it to him in a new way. In the ancient world, name changes meant massive transformation (see, for example, Genesis 17:5; 32:28). Peter's identity changed in that moment: the depth of his confession, regardless of all the curious questions still lingering after the words had left his lips, changed him. Granted, Peter still faced a journey filled with both trials and beauty. But he wouldn't walk that road as he had in the past.

It causes us to wonder—*does Jesus still change others' names?*

Does Jesus still radically reorient us to the world, filling us with his strength and the fruit of a new identity, shaping us with a brand-new name?

The path may begin with this simple question: *Who do you say that I am?*

QUESTIONS JOURNAL EXERCISE

Your Name Tag

Just as Jesus curiously engages the disciples' minds and hearts near Caesarea Philippi, he also offers us a chance to engage these two questions: Who do you say that I am? and Who do you think you are as a result?

This journal exercise requires some space and time, so set aside adequate room to reflect on and process the following questions. If you have access to a retreat center or other space that is designed for quiet, it would be helpful to use it in this exercise.

1. Take some time and read through Matthew 16:13-20. If you can, read it in multiple translations. Try to put yourself in the place of the disciples—feel their nervousness, their discomfort, and their hesitation. Hear them saying, "At least we know Jesus is here."

2. As you hear the question "Who do you say that I am?" try to honestly respond to it. Perhaps your response is an answer (You are . . .) or perhaps another question (What do you mean?). Let your responses come as they come, writing each one down.

3. Return to Jesus' first question, "Who do people say the Son of Man is?" We believe Jesus was referring to himself, so turn this question around so it applies to you. Who do people say you are? Who has "named" you throughout your life? Write down those names as you think of them—whether they are dark and painful or beautiful and life-giving—and keep them in front of you.

4. Let your curiosity flow, and ask the following question of Jesus: "Who do *you* say I am?" Spend some time in quiet listening for what the Spirit may have to say to you. What name is Jesus affirming in you? What name is Jesus changing? Are you being moved from "Simon" to "Peter"?

5. Take a moment and savor the healing, hope, encouragement, or even confusion that may come out of this time. Pray with thanksgiving for the question and the shift of identity that Jesus has brought into your life.

CHAPTER FIVE

a question of motivation

"Teach me thy ways, O Lord" is, like all prayers,
a rash one, and one I cannot but recommend.

ANNIE DILLARD

What must I do to inherit eternal life?

It isn't uncommon to find me leaning into our wide-open refrigerator and examining the contents.

"What are you looking for?" my wife will ask.

"Hey, what are you doing with this cheese?" I ask.

"Why?"

She's incredibly smart, and she realizes that I'm not just curious about the cheese. I have intentions, motivations, and plans are building up around my question. Behind the *what* of my question and the *how* of my asking lurks a quiet but powerful *why*.

I'm asking *because* I want to eat the cheese. It's a given, *because* I have issues saying no to cheese. She knows it. This is *how* I encounter cheese in general. So she asks why to find out what I'm after.

What. How. Why.

What is very factual—ideas, answers, and concepts—and *how* is very practical. The *why*, however, is the wellspring; it's the deep source that feeds the first two questions in every area of our lives.

Is it possible that in these three questions we find our true motivation when it comes to the life of faith? To explore that question, we're going to need a lawyer. And of course Jesus.

A Loaded Question

Jesus is questioned by "an expert in the law" (Luke 10:25). The lawyer has a very specific job: when everything is chaotic, remind people of the legal boundaries God beckons them to keep.

These experts were the great enforcers of the Jewish law, with deep threads of faithfulness and tradition woven into their souls. They knew and taught the directives of God that generation after generation kept the boats of simple people upright on a stormy, cultural sea.

To be clear, boundaries, laws, and guidelines aren't evil. Without basic instructions about hygiene, safety, and relationships, human babies will struggle and fail to grow.

When it comes to faith, we hunger for boundaries. We see the cultural complexity that sometimes strikes our faith, and we want to know what to do in response.

We want to know that we are walking well with God, if we in fact believe in him, and that we are both with him and also engaged in his good work. What are the markers for us—the things we look back on at the end of each day and say we did well or we didn't hit the mark? These markers become our motivation. They chart our course ahead. They are part of the great moral and ethical GPS; they often help us find our way in the world.

I notice that today we tend to look at laws with narrowed eyes. In Christian circles we say that we don't live by law but by grace and the Spirit, and we don't really need laws. Besides, the laws created Pharisees, right?

I agree. Yes, the law created tension, but it also created *beauty*. Celebrating holy days marking the historical movements of God, embracing the sabbath, and generously giving the first of your produce or livestock are all means toward *becoming* something. They create beautiful people.

I try to remember this during homework time in our house. It makes sense that while "everyone else" is outside doing something fun the schoolwork prisoner (also known as my child) would complain to her captors, despite the fact that she is becoming something good and beautiful in the world.

Laws can be the great *what* and *how* of God's life in the world.

For people of faith, *what* and *how* come from a great two-sided question: *What is God asking of us,* and *how do we live in a way that pleases God and makes sense of our world?*

The teacher, the expert in the law, asks Jesus a question: "Teacher . . . *what* must I do to inherit eternal life?" (Luke 10:25).

This is a common question for a teacher, a rabbi like Jesus.

The question is also built to press Jesus into a corner.

The text says the expert "stood up to test Jesus" (Luke 10:25), to push him, to open him up to public challenge. It was a vulnerable moment, the crowd and disciples watching to see what new insight Jesus had to offer on a tried and true body of commandments.

For the people of God, *what* you did and *how* you did it carried tremendous weight. The expert is asking Jesus a wide-open question filled with opportunities to miss something important, which leads to the first problem.

Getting It Done

Admittedly, I wasn't the best student in college. I was far more concerned with hanging around with my dorm tribe than studying. Or sleeping for that matter.

I can clearly remember waking up ten minutes before class, squirting some toothpaste in my mouth, and running across campus only to slump into a seat and resume dozing. A scholar doesn't rise from this kind of soil.

My primary motivations when it came to studies, with a few exceptions, were the following questions: What do I need to do to pass the class? and What do I need to do to graduate? or How do I get through this process? I took classes and completed assignments with this kind of intellectual minimalism, and as I look back now I realize how impoverished my mind and spirit were during that time in my life.

Is it possible that in our life of faith we have been so committed to the minimum *whats* and *hows* to "get right with God" that we're missing out on something much more difficult but also far brighter and more beautiful?

Have we surrendered the pursuit of the *best* of God for the *enough* of God? I admit there are difficult seasons when we subsist on God, when we fight through the valley of the shadow of death with only the rumor of God being with us (see Psalm 23), but as with all seasons, if it never ends it isn't a season.

The significant drawback to "getting it done" is simple: *it creates legalism.*

There's something about crisis, fear, and change that make us try to go back to the basics—to the most essential things—and *protect* ourselves. You can see this in the human body. We believe the best way to lose weight is not to eat, but our body has different ideas. When our body senses that we're not getting the calories, the fuel we need, it begins to store up fat to *protect* itself. Survival becomes the only thing that matters.

The Jewish people had come to a moment in their history when they were waiting for God to come and make all things right, to rebuild and reform the temple, to bring them back together as a nation, and to throw out all of those Roman squatters in the Promised Land. They sought the life they had been promised, the life that they dreamed of—*eternal life*, life forever and ever.

However, Israel's religious leaders sensed that obedience to the law, the fuel of God's people moving toward eternal life, was decaying, and therefore survival was critical. So they entered into spiritual starvation mode, storing up legal requirements and focusing deeply on *what* people needed to do and *how* they needed to do it.

The people had begun to move away from the law, away from their identity. For them, God had drifted from the center. The law was being compromised, so keeping it became spiritual gold to the religious leaders of the time.

Their motivation became making sure the deeds were done in the proper way, the actions completed, and the obligations fulfilled no matter what. This was the spiritual fat in their spiritually starving world.

Do we ever go to that place?

Do we become motivated by the *what* and *how* in order to stay out of trouble, keeping God happy with us? Making lists and checking them twice? Personally, I wouldn't mind more simplified lists of dos and don'ts, but therein lies the problem: something like parenting isn't a three-step process, and renewing a marriage takes a hundred steps every single day because on many of those steps we slide sideways or stumble backwards.

We aren't being formed for real life if we believe doing the right thing three times is all that it takes.

What if the problem of our lists and three-step processes isn't that they're evil but that they're simply cheap and limited visions compared to what Jesus has in mind?

Jesus knows the legal expert's plan, so he returns a question for a question.

Jesus responds, "What is written in the Law? . . . How do you read it?" (Luke 10:26).

Jesus takes the *what* and places it in a very *personal* context. How do *you* read it? It isn't just about the *what* of commandments, content, and facts. There's a layer beyond. These are *how* questions.

What would it sound like for this question to come to us too?

How do we read it? In our simple homes, surrounded by real family and real situations, how do we read it?

In our fears and reverences, believing God to be good but somewhat stern about his commandments, how do we read it?

Jesus isn't asking the expert in the law to *recite* the law back to him; Jesus is asking him what *he thinks the key to eternal life might be.*

Jesus' best questions come not through a direct query like we use in Google, but through exploration and processing. What if the curious step for us in this passage is to realize what *New York Times* writer Ben Greenman indicates? "By supplying answers to questions with such ruthless efficiency, the Internet cuts off the supply of an even more valuable commodity: productive frustration. Education [is] about filling [people] with questions that ripen, via deferral, into genuine interests."

The *how* question asks us to dig a bit deeper, moving from "what should we do" to "*how would we do that anyway?*"

From Information to Action

As someone who isn't mechanically inclined, most of my education on home improvement comes from YouTube. Recently, the pilot light went out on my hot water heater. The thought of working with a natural gas source and an open flame was frightening, so I sought wiser counsel before I blew up my home.

I went online and searched "how to light a pilot light on a hot water heater."

The search resulted in *thousands* of videos.

Each video had a *what*: this is gas, this is a flame, this is what you need to do. Each video had a *how*: steps, processes, and techniques to follow through on the *what*. This created a new question.

It was up to me, however, to take that instruction and ask, *Why* would I do it that way? Does this make sense in my house and with my particular type of water heater? It had to make sense in the real-life context of my house and equipment.

Just so you know, I didn't blow up the house.

But what if I had approached my hot water heater as a legalist? That is, my video teachers gave me the *what* and the *how*, so I just need to light the pilot without thinking. Legalism occurs when *what* and *how* become stronger than *why*. Which is problematic because *what* and *how* change, but *why* never does.

Here's an example. The church as a whole is struggling with a gender crisis. Many of us have been raised and cultivated to see church leadership as primarily a male role, and the female role is to support the males. We've been taught this is the design and desire of God.

In a curious twist, churches today are predominantly female in their congregational makeup. We have more female-led, single-parent households now than at any other time in history. We have more female executives and more females expressing leadership gifts in the public sector than ever before. Not nearly enough, mind you, but more.

The church has been living in the *what* and *how* passages on the gender issue—but what about the *why*?

Have we ever examined why those teachings are in Scripture? Have we thought critically about the *why* of male-only leadership for a first-century culture and, in turn, playfully and curiously examined whether that makes sense for a twenty-first-century culture?

Perhaps it is time for us to stop memorizing just the *content* of Scripture and begin to wrap our hands around the *context* as well. How do we move beyond the *what* of the text and into the *why* of who it's shaping us to be and toward a new *how* to live it out in our present-day world?

In exploring curiosity and how it shapes us, I've found a razor-sharp edge to the whole process. Often curiosity leads us to ask questions that are unpopular, and these rattle foundations that carry the weight of fragile structures and systems. We can see it on the faces of others as we ask the questions, or as we live them out.

Why questions are troublesome to *what* and *how* systems.

My own journey with curiosity has led me toward writers and thinkers that others in my faith community would find challenging if not downright heretical. They are writers and thinkers who ask hard questions. Writers, for example, who state the obvious about institutions like churches that habitually protect their own future over discovering where Jesus is headed and walking with him.

In the voices of people such as Richard Rohr, Shane Claiborne, and Ronald Rolheiser, I sensed a new brilliance—not intellectual brilliance but an illuminating light shining on things in a very clear way.

To stand in that well-lit place, however, I had to take a step away from some of my foundations and ask new questions. I didn't reject where I had come from, those teachers and preachers who helped build me from the ground up. I simply had to reassess what was most important, what was driving my pursuit of Jesus.

Why am I in this "Christian thing" anyway? Why am I here?

In his book *Tribes*, Seth Godin says, "A fundamentalist is a person who considers whether a fact is acceptable to his religion before he explores it. As opposed to a curious person who explores first and then considers whether or not he wants to accept the ramifications."

The process of becoming curious is the movement away from simply living by *what* and *how*, and moving into the beautifully ambiguous and possibility-laden world of God's *why* and all that comes with it.

What would it look like for us to live every moment of every day simply intoxicated by God's why? And what is that great *why* anyway?

Hearing the Why

The lawyer's response to Jesus' question is fairly standard Jewish language: "'Love the Lord your God with all your heart and with all your soul and with all your strength and with all your mind'; and, 'Love your neighbor as yourself'" (Luke 10:27).

The lawyer combines two texts, one from Deuteronomy 6:5 and one from Leviticus 19:18. In Jewish tradition Deuteronomy 6:5 is part of a prayer called the *Shema*, which means "to hear." The word didn't simply mean to register sound waves in our ears and our brains, it meant to take it in and do it. In other words, to hear is to *obey*. Not very specific, is it? Not exactly a plan. It says obey, but it doesn't say how. And there isn't really a *why*, is there?

We get some insight on all three questions through Jesus' response to the teacher: "You have answered correctly. . . . Do this and you will live" (Luke 10:28).

At this point, you can almost imagine an unspoken dialogue going on between Jesus and the teacher of the law.

Do what?

Love God with everything and love your neighbor as yourself.

How?

(*crickets chirping*)

In drawing the expert in, hearing his heart, and encouraging his response, Jesus is also pulling back the curtain on a deliciously troubling idea: the greatest commandment is all-consuming, but it's also nonspecific.

What are we to do in the daily interactions we all live? *What* and *how* don't make much difference if they fail to address the downright maddening complexity of our lives.

Should I let this person back in my life?

How do I know God's will for me in my sexuality, with all these questions swirling in my head?

How can I forgive that person?

Is it okay for me to be cremated?

Can I serve in the church if I'm divorced?

In Jesus' response to the expert, the word *correctly* comes from the Greek word *orthōs*, from which we get the word *orthodoxy*. Is it possible that to be truly orthodox is to love pervasively and without limits? Beyond that, is it really possible to love God with everything we have? Is it possible that this greatest commandment (see Matthew 22:38-40) is the great *why* that shapes our spirits into exactly what God had in mind?

Personally, I wrestle with loving God pervasively. I can love him with my mind, thinking and processing his grace and light, but the transition from head to heart and then to action is often bumpy and more often nonexistent. I know what to do with the realities of God that infuse my reality, but being motivated to actually do it often feels like taking the planet onto my shoulders.

How do I really love my neighbor as myself? (We'll do more with this in chapter six.)

I am still working through these questions, but when it comes to Jesus and the teacher of the law I am reminded of the many times we see Jesus reading the inscriptions on the hearts of those well-versed in the law. He can see their intentions, their motivations, their secret caverns.

Perhaps it's some sort of divine perception. Or perhaps he's simply examining the fruit of their lives. Either way, when he affirms the teacher of the law saying, "Do this and you will live," he leaves another question on the table: *Are you the kind of person who can do that?* You know the *what* of the law, and I've commissioned you to figure out the *how*, but are you intoxicated by the *why*? Are you committed to executing the steps of being transformed?

What if we began to look at the laws and commandments through the lens of *why*, not in terms of what we do but of who we're becoming?

Why We Run

In 2010, I decided to run the Chicago Marathon.

It was a time when my wife and I had made a commitment to be healthier. We had received some less-than-exciting news about our bloodwork, and needed to make some changes.

I needed something to help keep my motivation going.

With the advice of a friend, I searched the web for a marathon training plan and also registered for a 5K run (3.3 miles), just to get a feel for running a race. I began to follow the training plan, which didn't make sense to me at first. A marathon is 26.2 miles, but nowhere in the plan did it indicate that I needed to run 26.2 miles. Instead, you fill nearly eighteen weeks with short and longer-distance runs until your body is ready—until you are *formed*—for the real race.

So I ran. Every Saturday morning throughout a sweltering Chicago summer I plodded along on the pebble-paved trails of our local forest preserve. These were the long runs, reaching a maximum of twenty miles. Every day during the week, however, I did a smaller run between three and eight miles.

I filled water bottles at night; laid out my shorts and shirt, shoes and socks, and put my watch on top of everything so I would not forget it.

I rose before the sun, ran in both rain and wind, often wearing a reflective vest so as not to get hit by early morning drivers.

The reality is that 26.2 miles is far too complicated—too complex of a challenge for our muscular and skeletal systems—to simply *do*. You could wake up tomorrow, never having run that far, and try to run a marathon. But even if you make it you will likely have some long-term soreness and even injuries for your trouble.

We can't simply *do it*. We have to become the *kind of person* who does it.

How do we become people who would learn to live by love, both for God and others, as easily and naturally as breathing?

What if this is the real and meaty heart of spiritual formation? It seems Eugene Peterson is right when he says Christian spirituality

> does not present us with a moral code and tell us, "Live up to this"; nor does it set out a system of doctrine and say, "Think like this and you will live well." Instead, the way of Christian formation is to tell a story and in the telling to invite the hearer "Live into this—this is what it looks like to be human in this God-made and God-ruled world; this is what is involved in becoming and maturing as a human being."

When I tell the marathon story, most people ask *why*, and they aren't interested in my health transformation. Instead, they are asking why I would give myself to the rigors and physical torment of running *that far*, for *that long*, and *that often*.

I try to describe it as a process of *becoming* something. *Becoming* is the why. When it comes to faith, my desire to run is similar to the desire God draws us toward when

> He who is within us urges, by secret persuasion, to such an amazing Inward Life with Him, so that, firmly cleaving to Him, we always look out upon all the world through the sheen of the Inward Light, and react toward men spontaneously and joyously from this Inward Center.

We cannot train for a marathon, or engage in any long-term transformation, unless we are consumed by the *why*. Eternal life is the life of *why*—legalism is the life of *what* and *how*.

How does this happen? How do we become that kind of person?

Getting It Backwards

In his book *Start with Why*, business consultant and author Simon Sinek describes *why* as the driving factor for a successful business or product. Human beings, he says, have a powerful desire to feel like we *belong*, to feel like we're a part of something greater. He says,

> When a company clearly communicates their WHY, what they believe, and we believe what they believe, then we will sometimes go to extraordinary lengths to include those products or brands in our lives. *This is not because they are better, but because they become markers or symbols of the values and beliefs we hold dear.*

While the law and commandments in the story of faith don't necessarily inspire curiosity, Sinek's "defining the why" concept is important to this discussion. What if there is something almost magical at the heart of God's statutes and teachings?

Is it possible that the *why* of Jesus creates new markers or symbols that shape us into our true God-ordered selves?

What if we become deeply entangled in details and tasks because we're focused on *what* we're supposed to do and *how* we're supposed to do it, but in the meantime we've lost the *why* behind it all?

Many of Jesus' greatest teachings work through the same process. "Love your enemy" (Matthew 5:43-45), "remain in me" (John 15:1-5), and "do not worry about your life" (Luke 12:22-31) are beautiful, but they are also *open* in the way we apply them in the warp and woof of our own lives.

Jesus defeats legalism in our everyday life by reversing the order of the questions. Instead of beginning with the *what* and *how* of the commandments, he starts with the *why*.

Why should you love your enemy?

Why should you abide with me?

Why should you forgive as you've been forgiven?

You do these things because they are the heart and core of loving God with everything you have and loving your neighbor as yourself.

Notice the gap, however: *This is the why; the what and the how is up to you.*

This raises a question.

Is God really secure enough to let us engage the what and how? Is Jesus brave enough to invite people like the expert—people like us—to point the way forward? What if in our vocations, motivations, and actions we are invited to paint the strokes of obedience in our own colors? Barbara Brown Taylor speaks of her own vocation this way: "Whatever I decided to do for a living, it was not *what* I did but *how* I did it that mattered. God had suggested an overall purpose, but was not going to supply the particulars for me. If I wanted a life of meaning, then I was going to have to apply the purpose for myself."

Are we really to shape our lives around a God who more or less trusts us with the execution of his melodic plan for humanity? Does that reality cause us fear, uncertainty, and panic?

Jesus' response to the teacher is to "do this," but I wonder if a better way to read it is "Be the kind of person who loves God with everything and your neighbor as yourself. Eternal life will come along shortly."

Why bother with a pervasive, full-body love of God?

Why worry about loving our neighbor? They're negative, different, distant, and difficult.

What would it look like to recover Jesus' great *why* in our own lives—not obedience by force—and live by it?

How do we *learn* to live by the *why*?

We begin here: How do we inherit eternal life? What is the greatest commandment?

QUESTIONS JOURNAL EXERCISE

Grasping the Why

The questions in this chapter are some of the more challenging questions we deal with in our lives. Our *why*—our motivation—should be an area of disciplined, practiced, and curious exploration.

Jesus helps us simplify our focus on these questions to loving God and others. This journal exercise should help ask the questions that will help you live the *why* under complex expectations.

1. What questions did the chapter bring up for you regarding legalism and Jesus? What tensions or insecurities did you notice?

2. When you think about the *why* of the Great Commandment, what are the questions that come next?

3. When you think about the *how* and *what* questions, what still needs to be asked before you can act?

4. What questions have begun to come to the surface as you think about the history of your faith and the *why* that you were taught? What questions come to mind as you try to make peace with that past?

5. As you process these questions, I recommend reading *Falling Upward: Spirituality for the Two Halves of Life* by Richard Rohr. As you read, write down the questions that span between this book and that one. What similarities do you find?

CHAPTER SIX

a question of others

Perfect love of God with our heart, soul, mind and strength will not happen until we are no longer compelled to think about ourselves.

BERNARD OF CLAIRVAUX

Who is my neighbor?

Tim was one of the strangest people I had ever met, and I believe it was God's disruptive sense of humor that set Tim in the rental house next door.

When I was a high school student my family moved to a new house in town, and not long after our arrival Tim moved in. He drove an electric-blue, late-model Jeep, and you knew he was coming well in advance as the rumbling engine and pounding metal music arrived before he did.

Tim was heavyset, heavily tattooed, and alternated between hacking and coughing and drawing from a cigarette. Long strands of brown hair, tips dyed blonde, hung like greasy stalactites down his back and on his shoulders.

Tim *rarely* wore a shirt. He had a monitor lizard named Spike, and Tim regularly painted Spike's toenails red. The ceiling of his car was plastered with pornography. Tim had deep and strongly held convictions about the Bible and "modern-day preachers." He was, in some ways, a caricature of the rough and tumble journey.

How do I know all this? I know because Tim was my *neighbor*.

One night, starting in his driveway and then finishing four hours later in his kitchen, Tim and I learned about each other. He told me how he had seen the devil face to face. He also told me that when I became a "preacher" I had better hold that book out in front of me and not say anything that "ain't in the book." He confided that the drugs and dark exploits of his life had ruined his heart.

"Here, feel this," he said. He grabbed my hand and laid it— awkwardly for me—on his bare, clammy chest. I felt little in the way of a heartbeat.

"That sh-- is for real, man," he said. "That'll get me one day."

I found out a few years ago that his heart did indeed "get him." His meek and gentle wife came over and told us he had passed. Our lives intersected, a sixteen-year-old kid and a hard-knocks vagabond, but only for that moment.

Tim was, in the bravest language I know, a mess.

But he was my neighbor.

So who is your neighbor? More importantly, why does that matter?

A Person or a Cause?

In chapter five, we walked through an interaction between Jesus and an expert of the law. From that interaction we heard that eternal life is all about loving God with everything we have and loving our neighbor as ourselves. Jesus leaves the expert to curiously explore how to do that poetic work of God.

The conversation is not over.

The expert of the law used his conversation with Jesus as an opportunity to answer definitively and with great certainty *who* exactly counted as his neighbor. In an attempt to justify himself, he asked Jesus, "Who is my neighbor?" (Luke 10:29).

What is going on in the expert's mind? Notice, there's no clarifying question about loving God or how to love himself.

The question is, Who is my neighbor and how do I love my neighbor?

The word *justify* is important here. It comes from the word for "righteous" or "righteousness." The expert wanted to be "in the right" as far as his fulfillment of God's commands.

There is a significant problem with this kind of love. When the reason we love others is solely for our justification, we dehumanize them. They become "the poor," "the oppressed," "the lost."

Instead of being the *imago Dei*—the image of God—our own brothers and sisters created by God, they become a project to be marketed. They become a nameless, faceless, mass of generalities. They are not humans sharing in God's story who need to see rescue in action.

Has your love for neighbor ever become like a marketing project?

The In and the Out

Jesus responds to the expert's neighbor question by telling a story—a yarn he created to grasp the expert's curiosity and imagination, and point to something he couldn't have imagined. Something that he didn't want to imagine.

Plus, a spoiler alert: *Jesus never answers the man's question.*

According to Jesus, a man was walking along the Jericho Road from Jerusalem to Jericho. The road was notoriously violent; robbers and dark-souled men often inflicted harm on people coming down the road.

I had the chance to drive on such a road in Nairobi, Kenya. The Juja Road is a constant mashup of cars, animals, bikes, and pedestrians. My missionary friends said that at any moment people on the road may find themselves confronted by a weapon, and no one really blinks. People avoided Juja Road—just like they did the Jericho Road—whenever possible.

The man coming down Jericho Road was leaving Jerusalem, meaning he was likely a law-abiding Jewish man. He is ambushed by some non-law-abiding folks and left for dead.

Here we need heroes, or perhaps just one hero. We need someone who knows and does the right thing, coming to the man's rescue because that's the right thing to do.

Jesus says two men come down the road. These men were regal in their own eyes, but the cynics in Jesus' crowd would have groaned.

First, a priest. "Well, everyone knows you can't trust them," the crowd mutters.

And Jesus plays out the drama: the priest takes a wide berth and passes by the beaten man, proving the crowd right.

Did the crowd boo? Did they hiss?

Then a Levite comes. "Even worse," the crowd grumbles.

The Levite traces the sandal-prints of the priest and stays wide of the broken body, the fellow child of Yahweh writhing in agony, and goes on his way.

But what if they were doing the right thing?

The life and training, the formation, of the priest and the Levite taught them that blood made them unclean and unfit to carry out their priestly duties. Now the fact that they were coming *from* Jerusalem and were off the temple clock could have been a consideration, but it wasn't.

The law says *no* blood, so no blood for me, thank you. Staying clean here. Keeping the law, here. At least part of it.

It was hero time in the story. As Jesus wet his lips to speak, I imagine the crowd leaned in, waiting to hear who the hero would be.

Say someone like me, some in the crowd thought. Someone simple. Someone with a wife and family. Someone who barely scrapes by should be the hero. A good, observant, struggling, and oppressed Jewish man or woman like me. It's about time someone like me saved the day.

Instead, Jesus stole the breath of the crowd and said, "But a Samaritan, as he traveled, came where the man was; and when he saw him, he took pity on him" (Luke 10:33).

Samaritans, in the eyes of the Jewish people, were less than low class. They were no class. Samaritans were Jewish impostors with questionable family origins. They didn't talk like the Jews talked, worship where they worshiped, or obey all the laws Jews obeyed. They didn't think, speak, smell, or live like Jews did.

We know this character, don't we?

The person we see in an airport and it makes us nervous.

The person we've been raised to believe is lazy, deceitful, and so on.

The person we hope we don't have to sit next to on the train.

The person who lives in that neighborhood where we lock our doors when we drive through.

The person whose politics are not like ours.

The person who doesn't worship like we do.

The person who has a different sexual orientation than we do.

The person who has committed *that* crime.

Here we need to pause and ask a question: What happens when Jesus makes our enemy the hero of the story? Is our journey with Jesus shaping us for this tremendous shift?

Justice for Samaritans

The Samaritan stops and attends to the Jewish man: tearing his own garment and tying the beaten man's wounds. Bearing the man's protest, the Samaritan lifts him gently but forcefully onto his own animal.

He takes him to a local inn. Placing him on an open bed, the Samaritan promises to settle whatever bills it takes to bring this man to health. Whatever it takes. The Scripture says the man was near death (Luke 10:30)—this could be quite a bill.

Stop here and imagine being a Samaritan and hearing about this event. You have lived your entire life pushed down, shoved away, and ridiculed by Jewish people. You could say the beaten man had it coming to him. This was justice being done.

Justice? Hmm.

The word for *righteousness* can also be translated "justice"—both the Hebrew and the Greek words carry the dual translation of "justice" and "righteousness."

The Samaritan wasn't right in the eyes of his people. He didn't have a law that required him to do anything. The priest and the Levite were right by their people, obeying a law that had been passed down for generations. The Samaritan was the *other*—the outcast, the villain, the enemy—so what does that do to our thoughts on love and justice?

We, like the original hearers, are likely processing a great deal of chaos when it comes to others.

Love Is Chaos

I had coffee with a friend who was seeking spiritual direction. We talked about the last few years of his life and what God had been shaping in him. He had come to a place where some of the details—the *what* and *how* (see chap. 5)—that had built and energized his faith were starting to shake loose. He was questioning, he was challenging, and some people close to him were wondering if he was a Christian at all.

There was a lot of chaos in his life, and as we journeyed through spiritual direction we came to terms with the fact that pursuing *why* rather than *what* or *how* was filled with chaos. Because he had grown up in the church, he had to get past the idea that "something needs to be fixed."

Eventually he learned that nothing needs to be fixed. It's all part of the deal: chaos is part of walking with God. Being righteous—living out of God's great *why*—can include chaos. The good Samaritan story threw a bunch of law-keeping folks into total chaos. It was okay. Embrace it. It's part of life.

The teacher of the law who tested Jesus didn't stop at knowing the greatest commandment, because he wanted to *safely order his world with God.*

So where is this story headed with the Samaritan on Jericho Road? Where is it taking you and me as we love our neighbors?

Knowing Your Neighbor

In college I had the opportunity to work in inner-city Washington, DC, for a week, serving in a variety of homeless shelters and social service agencies. We, a shoulder-to-shoulder gang of twenty-somethings, were serving in a soup kitchen, and as the line grew we began to think about efficiency. We started making sandwiches ahead of time, layering meat, cheese, and mustard on the open rolls and wrapping them neatly. We felt very proud of being both compassionate and efficient.

That is, until a grizzled man with an impenetrable beard asked, "Does this have mustard on it?"

"Yes it does," we replied.

"Yuck. I don't want that. What else do you have?"

It was not my greatest moment, to be sure, but the first thought that came to mind was *You're here because you're hungry, and you want to quibble over condiments?*

What are our assumptions about the *other*, about our neighbor?

Curiosity is critical in loving our neighbor because it moves us beyond the *other* as "they" or "those people," and it restores their humanity back because we *know* them.

What if the greatest way to love is to be formed into the kind of person who cares enough about the other to know whether they want mustard or not?

Are we afraid to know our neighbors because we'd have to accept and engage in their messy lives—we'd have to learn preferences, likes, dislikes, and opinions, which might be different from our own?

Perhaps keeping the greatest commandment, then, is as much about learning the gritty lives of those we don't know (or fear) as it is about exploring the terrifying beauty of God.

The Question of Other

The power of Jesus' story comes from one critical element—*fear*. Fear of the unknown, the other, the different and the strange, drives people to make all sorts of unwise decisions.

As I write this, the world is alive with fear. Racial struggles in the United States, terrorist attacks in Iraq, Afghanistan, France, and Germany, and a US presidential election that looks more like a TV reality show than democracy.

Underneath all of the rhetoric and news headlines, what stands? What is bubbling below the surface? In my mind, I see *fear*. Experts tell us that the majority of political campaigns tap into three emotional streams—*fear*, *uncertainty*, and *doubt*, or FUD for short. The cultivation and captivation of FUD evokes a response. We move, we vote, we spend or save money largely based on FUD.

But what kind of playmates are FUD and the Great Commandment?

Writer Elizabeth Gilbert says that "fear is the enemy of curiosity." I tend to agree, but fear is relatively easy to set aside when it's localized in ourselves and our little cosmos.

I'm anxious about my marriage. Trust God, fear not.

I don't know how this exam is going to go. Trust God, let him calm you.

What about my health? He is the Great Physician.

But what about others?

What if the point of Jesus' teaching on the Great Commandment reveals that the reason we must love God and our neighbor is that we are inherently a fearful people?

What if the problem of racism is rooted in our hereditary fear of knowing the *other* deeply enough to love them well?

Can we become curious about the active struggle within us when it comes to "who is my neighbor" without honestly assessing our own struggle to *be* a neighbor to them?

Loving God with everything we have implies that we chase after *knowing* God—his character, desires, and personal contours. If the "second is like it," then the command to love our neighbor must go beyond the legal expert's neighbor-as-target mentality and pursue actually knowing our neighbor.

As Jean Vanier says, "We will continue to despise people until we have recognized, loved, and accepted what is despicable in ourselves."

The teacher of the law is confronted with a deeply broken part of himself. We, if we become curious about the *other*, are also confronted with a broken part of ourselves.

I learned to care about a homeless man's mustard aversion. To me, he was a target to be catered to rather than a person to be known. Yet I knew by heart the passage: "Whatever you did for one of the least of these brothers and sisters of mine, you did for me" (Matthew 25:40). The way we love our neighbor should match the way we love ourselves and the way we desire to love Jesus.

Speaker and writer Bob Goff said, "If you want to know the condition of your heart, look at how you treat those you disagree with."

This examination is relatively easy. We can notice the churning viscera of our stomachs and realize what we've been formed into. We can look at our social-media footprint and see evidence of the transformed life, or the lack thereof. Who do we love in what we share, like, and retweet?

To love is to move past fear, which drives our suspicion of the *other*, fear that promotes classism and discrimination. We develop the curiosity to ask more brilliant questions, the first and foremost being: *Do we really know those we claim to love?*

What do we risk when we love our neighbors?

Loving the Other with Lunch

Recently my family and I took a trip to Anaheim, California, for a conference. During our stay we visited the Crystal Cathedral, now called the Christ Cathedral.

The cathedral was being renovated, so we weren't able to go in, but the grounds were beautiful. With the sharp, clean sun on our shoulders, we walked throughout the campus and were captivated by the many sculptures highlighting Jesus' life. (You may be thinking, *You know, they have beaches in Southern California, Casey.* We did that too, trust me.)

One sculpture in particular captured my daughter's attention. Jesus stood, with that deep smile you can only imagine coming from someone who had harnessed a childlike faith, with a child on his left and two disciples on his right. The child in the sculpture held a basket of loaves and fish. The sculpture was itself a miracle—a scene cut from mineral earth—naming a miracle, the feeding of the multitudes with an incredibly small inventory.

As we walked away, my daughter spoke up, "That was a big deal, you know!"

"Yep," I replied. "Multiplying the little for the many."

"No," she corrected. "It was a big deal for the little boy."

"Why?" I asked. She had me on this one.

"It was that little boy's lunch, and he just gave it away. What if it never came back?"

Is there a more beautiful moment than when a child's curiosity turns a beloved text on its head and brings a new perspective into the light?

My wife stepped in and said, "You know, I guess sometimes we can see the miracle but miss the sacrifice."

I started taking notes.

The Samaritan in Jesus' story risked his own harm: What if the man lying beside the road was a robber's setup to ambush others? This was a common practice on the Jericho Road.

He risked his own resources: How bad was this man's condition? How much money would it take to get him back to health?

He risked his own reputation: What happens when the other Samaritans see you with a Jew, the ones who hate, oppress, and insult you?

What do we risk when it comes to the *orthodoxy of love*, both knowing and loving our neighbor? Do we risk losing our tribe, our doctrinal brothers and sisters? Do we risk losing our staunch political, social, and economic positions?

Is all the risk worth it, just for the sake of love? Can we curiously assess how much our fear of risk limits our ability to love as Jesus invites us to love?

Ignoring and Answering the Question

Jesus turns to the astonished expert in the law and delivers the crescendo: "Which of these three do you think was a neighbor to the man who fell into the hands of robbers?" (Luke 10:36).

Remember, the lawyer asked, "Who is my neighbor?" He is left with only one response, an unexpected answer to his own question: The expert in the law replied, "The one who had mercy on him."

Jesus said, "Go and do likewise" (v. 37).

Jesus answered with a question of his own, pulling the expert into a curious pursuit that he wasn't expecting. *Don't worry about who your neighbor is, my friend. This is what a neighbor looks like.*

Being a neighbor means being consumed by the *why*. Don't worry about definitions, become the miracle who knows how to risk.

Don't find a person. Be a person. That's the most important thing.

What would it look like to be a person who loves without thinking of the implications, to embrace the chaos and fear and messiness of the other? What would it look like to sacrifice in such a way that the miraculous would haphazardly spill out on the world?

I suggest we begin here: Who is your neighbor?

QUESTIONS JOURNAL EXERCISE

Are There Others?

The question of the *other*—our neighbors, both the difficult and demanding, familiar and foreign—is central to this chapter. I hope I painted a picture of what love for others looks like in the messiness of real life. The *how* is something we need to think about, which is the purpose of the following exercise.

1. As you read the story of the lawyer and the Samaritan, what did you feel was left unanswered or unspoken? What unanswered questions were left when the chapter ended?

2. Who came to mind as you thought about your *others*? As you picture them, what do you need to know about them in order to love them?

3. What are some unanswered questions you have about the risk involved in loving others well? What would you need to know before stepping into the risk-filled, chaotic act of loving your neighbor?

4. What questions remain for you about how you love yourself? And how do those affect the way you love your neighbor?

5. Imagine that the man beaten by the roadside could talk with you today. What questions would you want to ask him? What would you ask the Samaritan man?

a question
of love and failure

Because God lovingly leads us to face our wounds and
weaknesses, there is always the danger we will cut and run
at the moment we most need to stay and endure.

BEN BARCZI

Do you love me?

Our good friends Jon and Jennifer adopted a child from China. Iris is a very small, very mobile smile machine. With an uncharacteristically deep Janis Joplin-esque voice, she is a gift to the life of their family and anyone she meets.

One night over good wine and Italian food, we talked about raising and disciplining our kids. They shared that when Iris gets into trouble, she asks, "Are you going to put me up for adoption?" Iris has lived in the United States with her new family for several years now, but the old reality still hangs heavy on her little mind.

"Do you love me?" Iris inquires with every single tear.

Jennifer's response is classic. "It's illegal to put kids up for adoption here in the States," she quips. Then she follows with, "We've talked about this, how long will I be your mom?"

"Forever," Iris squeaks through watery mouth and eyes.

Iris's question wasn't a question of whether she'd have to change her address and live somewhere else.

It was a question of love.

We ask these questions of the world, of our family, and of our friends every single day. When we hear that affirmative response, we're strengthened. I grew up with parents who frequently told me they loved me, and I realize now what a great gift that was, because many haven't grown up with that word spoken over their daily world.

Love gives us roots, develops a sense of belonging, and places us in relationship with ourselves, with others, and with the world at large. The kind of love we are searching for is what Paul describes in 1 Corinthians 13. If you've been to a wedding recently you have heard these words:

> Love is patient and kind. Love is not jealous or boastful or proud or rude. It does not demand its own way. It is not irritable, and it keeps no record of being wronged. It does not rejoice about injustice but rejoices whenever the truth wins out. Love never gives up, never loses faith, is always hopeful, and endures through every circumstance. (1 Corinthians 13:4-7 NLT)

If love endures through every circumstance, what about when we fail to see it through? Can love live through failure?

In other words, how is love still alive when we fail: When we are shamed, become cynical, and doubt ourselves because of what we have done or left undone? What's more, is curiosity even *helpful* amid the stark pain of failure?

In the Gospel of John, Jesus asks Peter, "Do you love me?" The strange thing is that he asks *after* a moment of great failure on Peter's part. What might be hidden in this question of love?

When Nothing Is Biting

The lake was calm, too calm considering the storm going on in the hearts of the disciples. Jesus had died and reappeared to the disciples, but Peter sat stoically and unmoving at the bow of the boat (see John 21:1-14).

He had become anxious the evening prior, his hands twitching with the need for work and distraction, so he and some of the other disciples had gone fishing. They caught nothing, but the overnight trip gave Peter plenty of time to meditate on what had happened in the last month or so.

Jesus had commended Peter and given him the name Rock (Matthew 16:13-20). Jesus even made a promise about a revolutionary people being built on the ground of Peter's confession. Peter smiled at this recollection in the salt-kissed darkness. The smile faded however when he remembered the moments after the confession: Jesus had called Peter "the tempter" when Peter questioned Jesus' warning of conspiracy, capture, and execution (Matthew 16:21-28). Then, in gruesome scenes, everything came to pass just as Jesus had said. The arrest. The betrayal. The trial and crucifixion.

We know the sting of betrayal. We know it going both ways, neither better to give nor to receive. We have failed, and we *have been* failed. We have denied, and have been denied. The beautiful wreck of our humanity allows us to both inflict and receive pain.

Peter was afraid when Jesus was arrested. He acted in fear when asked if he was with Jesus. He denied even knowing Jesus. It seemed the Rock had crumbled.

Peter failed to love, so it seems. So what would love do with failure now? Is there hope for something beautiful to rise from these ashes?

Peter pulled on the nets, drawing them over the side of the boat. Nothing. An empty net and an empty stomach were present realities as the sun came up. I wonder if somewhere a rooster crowed, just within the range of Peter hearing, and he shook his head.

On the shore, a voice cracked through the new day's orange glow. "Did you catch anything?" the voice asked. Peter and his companions groaned, then shouted, "No. No luck."

"Did you try the other side?" the voice asked.

"Did we try the other side? Who does this guy think he is?" they grumbled.

"Put a net over there," the voice said. "See what happens."

This had happened before: a voice called out from the shore, nets were cast, and fish *voluntarily* entered the nets. In that moment, Peter had found himself at the feet of Jesus, in awe and worship (Luke 5:6-11).

This day, just as in the one before, the nets were cast and fish came in droves.

"Jesus," John blurted out. "It has to be Jesus."

Typically when men fished in first-century Galilee, they stripped down to their bare necessities when it came to clothing. It was achingly hot in the middle of the water, and, frankly, getting your outer garments wet was a hassle.

However, it was disrespectful to come before someone you loved and honored without your outer garments on, so Peter made a quick wardrobe choice. He wrapped his outer garment around him and leapt headfirst into the water, swimming to the beach where Jesus was.

If Peter really believed it was Jesus, there had to be some conflict going on as he made that swim. He was overjoyed that it was true—bountifully true. The resurrection was indeed real and his own betrayal was not final.

Yet Peter was also swimming toward the man he had promised to never leave and always support, the man Peter had denied three times at a moment when the utmost act of love would have been to fall on the sword with Jesus.

Was this swim worth it to Peter for the sheer possibility of erasing his failure?

Finding Curiosity in Failure

What happens *after* our moments of failure? If we had the opportunity to move toward a moment that might be uncomfortable or tense, what would drive us to *swim* toward it with reckless abandon? What quality would make us want to do that?

Part of our formation as curious children of God is learning how to understand and embrace our failures as part of who we *are* and at the same time *repent* of our old ways of seeing failure.

To embrace where we are broken, where we make grand promises and yet fail to keep them, is part of learning love's new song. The story of Peter gives us a way forward and new questions to ask along the way.

I'll never forget the first time I had to apologize to my daughter. She was still small, and I had failed to keep my end of a commitment to her. I brought myself to my child, the picture of innocence, having failed her at something seemingly insignificant. I am the one she should be able to trust, one who should always have her best in mind and always act rightly and lovingly. Honestly, I thought through the ways I could use my adult reasoning to rationalize the whole thing away.

I confess I thought about bribery with ice cream.

But I had to mend that moment, showing her that she is a blessing worthy of love and attention. Even that slight had the potential to dissipate into the rest of the moments of her life.

I admitted my failure so she could know how much she is loved. I don't always do that. There is reflexivity to failure and love, they walk closer than we might imagine. We discover the one within the other, failing the ones we love and loving the ones who fail us. Her small voice came through, both soft and razor-sharp:

It's okay, Daddy.

I admitted that I'm not God. I agreed with Jesus in that moment that no one is good but God (Mark 10:18), and in return I was given a hug, a smile, a soft cheek, and grace beyond her years.

Love like Paul describes in 1 Corinthians 13 came to life in that very moment. In the moment of my failure, regardless of how small, love came in. I was a dad who had failed, and all was made well through the love that innocents carry.

The Beach at Sunrise

When Peter and the rest of the disciples arrived on shore, they found Jesus grilling fish and welcoming them—all of them—to do the most human and life-giving thing possible: to eat.

Love here is being painted new and bright. Love is the steadfastness of Jesus returning for a simple meal after a miraculous catch of fish that relieved the disciples of their various hungers. This is an ordinary happening, a very loving act done on Jesus' behalf for the men who had at one point walked with him.

In my moments of failure I have found Jesus to be far less spectacular than he is kind and common. Frankly I'm not the first to recognize when I've failed or that I have failed at all. When I know my failure and admit it to someone, the words, actions, and attention of those I have wounded are beyond divine.

The moment of God's forgiveness isn't built on fireworks and epiphany but solid, simple, and enduring goodness: the kind of goodness we might find in a meal with those we love. The kind of goodness that we find in simply being with a dear friend or loved one.

After the meal, the disciples reclined at ease with Jesus. With the juice of fish drying on their beards, a strange lightness had come into their voices.

It was that luxury of free men living with the liberating King, resting at his side, overjoyed to see his face and hear his voice. Peter was uneasy, however.

This is too comfortable. There's a lot between us right now.

Jesus sees Peter standing off at a distance, furiously rubbing his knuckles into his bearded chin. Peter's brow is creased and his eyes narrowed from stress and pain, but Jesus lays a powerful and gentle hand on Peter's shoulder and asks, "Simon son of John, do you love me?" (John 21:15).

Jesus asks this question two more times. He seems to be inviting Peter, and in some way you and me, to a discussion. In the midst of failure, Jesus levels the ground for Peter to stand on. Jesus' love for Peter is not in question here. Jesus is simply present.

In that moment of presence, Jesus didn't need to fix Peter. He didn't say, "Let's work on that denial thing, shall we?" In the midst of our failures, Jesus, who shapes us through his Spirit, simply *comes*.

He is present and asks, "Do you love me?" He isn't accusing, just present and searching. It's hard to miss the parallel imagery of God walking in the Garden, searching for Adam and Eve, asking, "Where are you?" (Genesis 3:9).

Jesus is engaging Peter's curiosity, opening his eyes. Jesus' question is not designed to pierce Peter's spirit—it's much more subtle and soul-shaping. As David Benner says, "Jesus asked [Peter] three times if he loved him. . . . This gave Peter three chances to declare his love—one for each denial. Jesus' response was to repeat his invitation for Peter to follow him, precisely the same invitation that had begun their relationship."

Peter is *invited* to take the lead in this discussion. Why?

Modern therapy gives us a picture that helps. After dealing with a particularly difficult session, eminent therapist Carl Rogers gave up his standard techniques and let the mother of a troubled young man talk without his interfering or suggesting change.

After this session Rogers said, "It began to occur to me that unless I had a need to demonstrate my own cleverness and learning, I would do better to rely upon the client for the direction of movement in the process."

What if Jesus, in the midst of our failure, shows us love by inviting us to participate in our redemption? What if he welcomes us to direct and guide the process, all the while calling us forward with the rich voice that has not been altered by our misdeeds and missteps?

Relying on Jesus' presence, Peter listened and responded. He participated. He ached at Jesus' every question, he winced as the questions compounded (John 21:17), but Jesus didn't move. He stayed near, lovingly watching Peter move closer to him.

What if when we fail those we love—when we fail to engage that authentic self that God is drawing to the surface—Jesus is near? He invites us to participate in our own restoration.

A Practice for the Process

One important spiritual practice, if we are curious enough to ask the necessary questions, is to embrace and give away our story of failure. We take time to look back over our journey and ask, Where is a moment when I failed? While this seems like a dangerous practice, as we walk with Jesus and are formed by him we begin to get a healthier sense of where our failures fit in the greater picture.

We capture one point in time, one particular story of failure, and we begin to retell it to ourselves.

It may be helpful to reflect on Psalm 51 as we wrestle with our story. David's great reflection on his own failure cries out:

> Create in me a clean heart, O God,
>> and put a new and right spirit within me.
> Do not cast me away from your presence,
>> and do not take your holy spirit from me.
> Restore to me the joy of your salvation,
>> and sustain in me a willing spirit. (Psalm 51:10-12 NRSV)

Into the midst of failure, David welcomes joy and a clean heart. He claims ownership of his story and in doing so creates space for the love of God to flow in, clean and pure. Along with Brother Lawrence, in that very moment we see that "This King, full of mercy and goodness, very far from chastising me, embraces me with love, makes me eat at His table, serves me with His own hands, gives me the key of His treasures."

What God Looks Like

When I was the pastor at a small rural church, we decided to do a vow renewal ceremony within our regular worship service. I had been teaching on the covenant of marriage, and I let the couples in our church know that we would be inviting them forward all at once to renew their vows.

Since our church was small, we had several people doing more than one thing at a time. A few of the husbands who wanted to take part in the vow renewal were downstairs leading our children's service. At the moment when I asked people to come forward, someone slipped down the stairs and told the husbands to come up. After that, they could return to songs and games and all the assorted kids' church activities.

One by one they came up the stairs, down the aisle, and joined with their wives. I began the vows with the wives, going through the covenant devotion and ending with, "If so answer, 'I do.'" After the wives responded, I prayed. Then the couples returned to their seats or to the basement.

Only later did someone kindly and sharply say, "So, are the guys off the hook for the vows?" I had never given the men a chance to make their vows.

Oh my.

The feeling that something significant has been forgotten, something that contributes to the value and goodness of a moment, is painful. The rest of this failure story is for another time. The point is, as we read John 21, something is missing.

Jesus neglects to do something in the Peter story, and it tells us a great deal about God.

I never noticed it, honestly, until I became curious about how the text unfolds. Jesus never commands Peter to repent. He doesn't call for confession. Peter also never asks for forgiveness. Jesus simply asks if Peter loves him, three times.

What haunts me about the three love questions is that they are meant to *restore* Peter. Jesus is engaging Peter's curiosity as a way of giving Peter back what seems to be lost and wasted.

For some of us, our picture of Jesus (and in turn, of God) is challenged here. If we see God as the authoritative hammer-wielding type, this makes no sense. We believe God is going to make Peter squirm. He failed, and now the moment has come for the ruthless love of contrition, confession, forgiveness, and repentance. "Sinners in the hands of an angry God," as Jonathan Edwards's classic sermon proclaims. Certainly denying Jesus at the point of his trial would draw the anger of God?

Jesus is going to make certain that Peter understands exactly what he has done by punishing him. Or so we think.

Jesus' three questions appear to be gentle even as they sting Peter's conscience. Jesus doesn't invite any of us to experience the love of God only to whip it away from us because our minds are still clunking around in the garage of shame and self-centeredness.

God did not love the world through Jesus *after* the world had filed the adequate paperwork for repentance. God loved the world *before* he sent his Son (see John 3:16).

As a spiritual director, I walk with people who fail. Some of them confess their struggle and take great strides at restoration. They walk with a limp—their hips out of socket from wrestling with God and others—never to be the same again. They wrestle with shame, the story of failure as an identity rather than an action, for the rest of their days. They do find a measure of life too.

The catalyst for change as we wrestle with our failures and the accompanying shame is to curiously engage with the image of God alive in our minds. In the words of Richard Rohr, "Our image of God makes us."

Curiosity, when it comes to our failure, has the potential to open new understandings of who God is and *isn't*. Why bother revisiting failure, why bother being curious about it? If God is one who punishes fully and completely, there's no reason to return to the scene of the crime. But what if Peter's story shows us something different?

Jesus' words to Peter suggest that God can be *found* in our failures, and in finding him there we discover a new and more potent image of the One who creates and calls.

What if Jesus truly *is* what God looks like—God's invisible character made visible (Colossians 1:15-23)? Can we embrace a Jesus who doesn't demand righteous behavior to atone for our failures? What if instead we are invited to explore the implications of our failures with Jesus, free of shame?

What if in this wild kingdom of God there is a way for us to be restored without a tongue-lashing from the divine? What if our soul is shaped to receive our failures in front of God, with this reality in mind? What would happen *next*?

What if we could wake up every morning and (in our minds) stand on the beach with Jesus? The previous day is filled with moments of love and neglect, selfishness and service, grace and legalism. As we reflect on the day behind us, scenarios unfold.

We hoarded our time out of fear of that person who drains us emotionally and spiritually.

We took a few deep breaths and searched the eyes of our child to see the image of God, filtered through our own DNA, staring back at us, and we realized that they aren't working off some devious script to ruin our lives. They merely are *a teenager*.

We spent some time in the quiet of our mind wondering about our own value to the world. We struggled to sense the love of our spouse or significant other, trying to navigate their words and actions to get to the heart of what they were laying on the table before us.

Into each of these situations, as we examine a day gone by, Jesus speaks softly and quietly—*Do you love me?* In the middle of the fray, are you being drawn to and shaped by this image of unconditional love, which helps you learn to live those strands of your day *differently*?

Meet Me Where I Am

Jesus engages Peter's shame with one question: "Peter, do you love me?" but then transitions to a command, "Feed my sheep" (John 21:15, 16, 17).

This is Jesus' way of reintegrating Peter—and us. Shame at our failure is tearing us to bits, so Jesus begins to put things back together. There is so much more goodness left for us to give to the world. What else might we do together, he says, when you find yourself whole again?

As I welcome you back to me, I am also at work putting things back together in your soul. Your mind, heart, and hands need to rediscover their beautiful rhythms and habits. I have a place for you in the world, and this moment of failure will shape you for it.

In the story behind Peter's story we often forget that when Jesus was crucified, the disciples fled for their lives out of fear of the Romans and the Jewish leaders. Peter was courageous enough to stay close, within earshot of Jesus' accusers, when others had run away. The disciples knew that to be identified with Jesus was to go with him through the fire. Peter went anyway.

Peter's denial in the courtyard likely kept him *alive*. What a strange thought! If Peter hadn't denied Jesus, he too may have been killed or tortured and imprisoned.

Better to take care of all the riffraff at once, the authorities would have reasoned.

Had Peter been executed at that moment, anything linked to Peter throughout the early church would be gone. The books of 1-2 Peter and the wisdom of knowing we are "living stones . . . being built into a spiritual house" (1 Peter 2:5) would never have been written. The stories of Peter and John in Acts, along with the sermon of Pentecost (Acts 2), would be washed away with a quick swipe of an unjust hand.

Peter had great work, poetic and beautiful work, left to do in the world. Without reintegration, without restoring and reengaging him in the script of God's great story, what wisdom would be missing from our world?

Is it possible that we can be formed even through our greatest failure, and that our failure could actually be a catalyst for great goodness? Alice Fryling observes, "Our perception of success and failure may, in fact be inaccurate. . . . Perhaps the almighty God has chosen to work through us without letting us know. We may find out years later that what we saw as failure was actually God's success."

Could the moment when we were least loving, least gracious, and even intentionally destructive serve as a structure on which God will build something more beautiful? What if our failure is actually *forming* us instead of *deforming* us?

In the church where I serve, I see beautiful things coming out of past failures. New stories being told from old tragedies become gifts, the tender work of stewarding God's "grace in its various forms" (1 Peter 4:10).

Those who have overcome addiction are shaping those who are dealing with addiction.

Those who have misused their financial resources and come through the ruins are now serving as sage guides for those who walk the same jagged pathways.

Those who have tossed live grenades into their relationships become mentors as they bring the tatters of their marriage together and walk forward no matter what.

We begin to realize that through love "in all things God works for the good of those who love him, who have been called according to his purpose" (Romans 8:28). We then have to step back for a moment and realize that our failures are actually moments for goodness and growth. So much is lost when we allow the story of shame to eviscerate our lives instead of becoming tools for the graceful formation of our work in the world.

Yes, there are consequences, and situations may never return to the way they were, but beyond that there is the opportunity for God to bring redemption to our seemingly irredeemable failures. The miraculous mystery then is how our failures, owned and embraced, can bring hope to others who are failing with us.

How does this happen?

Humility and Hope

Thomas Kelly says, "Unless the willingness is present to be stripped of our last earthly dignity and hope, and yet still praise him, we have no message in this our day of refugees, bodily and spiritual." What if failure shapes us into great messengers?

Honestly, Peter wasn't expecting to be reengaged in shepherding the flock.

Jesus once said, "I am the good shepherd. . . . My sheep listen to my voice" (John 10:11, 27). Is the Chief Shepherd (1 Peter 5:4) actually empowering the man who denied him, saying, "I'm leaving you the rod and the staff. I'm leaving you with the task of caring for my people"?

You, Simon son of John, who betrayed me, I'm giving you a gift. A trust. A task.

The lambs are gentle, they need a steady hand that will stick with them and love them well. You—you're the one I want for this task.

"Feed my lambs," Jesus repeats.

Peter's edginess is thinning. A softened look is in his eyes as Jesus moves again toward him with a task. He uses a different word here, not *lambs* but *sheep*. This is the herd, a great many, a multitude. Caring for a few lambs is one thing, but Peter is being given a great task.

Part of the great movement of restoration and reintegration is to be given back our purpose, our function, and our role in the work of God set aside for us in the world. We have to be shaped for that. Our souls must take on the shape that allows us to walk humbly into the next chapter of life.

Is it possible that the more closely we embrace our failures in front of Jesus, the more we are given in the way of grace and stewardship? Is Jesus looking for those who have failed and own their failure to be the ambassadors, the bearers of his kingdom?

The Great Renovation

Recently, our neighbor died. He was an older divorced man living alone save for two large and excitable Dobermans. The dogs were his family, he said. He had lost his job at the age of seventy, and he was living on Social Security and whatever other assistance he could find.

His house had fallen into ruin: partly from his own use, partly from the house being inhabited by two giant dogs, and partly from a lack of resources to do anything about it. Besides, a house built in the 1950s that isn't regularly repaired inevitably begins to fall apart.

When he died, his house was purchased for pennies by another neighbor who began the work of renewing and remodeling it. We watched as a dumpster was delivered and men in white jumpsuits and oxygen masks removed items from the house. Then we heard walls being demolished and saw the roof being torn off and replaced.

Then the outer walls were attacked, leaving nothing but studs and bare subfloor standing against the early spring sunlight. One day I saw the neighbor who purchased the house and asked him how the project was going.

"The whole place was ruined," he said. "We had to go down to the plates and start again." They replaced the rotting floors, the decaying studs, and the moldy chipped window frames.

Over the following months, we watched as the house was completely redone from the inside out. It became something different, something visually beautiful and whole. However, we continued to tell the old story: we still called it "Ralph's house."

Sometimes, when lives have fallen into such disrepair, for whatever reason, when they have dulled to a dingy brown, when they have let old failures and habits go that begged for mending and attention, the only way to salvage them is to start from the beginning.

We take a hammer to the things we thought would forever haunt us—those repeated failures we try so hard to avoid, those failures that reappear on the faces of our family members or friends—and we surrender our care of them. We are responsible, but we are not capable. The graceful gaze and hand of Jesus is needed at that moment, so he comes and stands on those decaying floorboards.

This isn't punishment; it's *restoration*. The events of the past few days had *deformed* Peter, distorting the deeper vision God had for this bombastic fisherman. Things needed to go back to the beginning.

For Jesus, Peter's failure is not an obstacle to Peter's restoration but an integral piece. In our stories, failure is the moment when we fall headlong into the skilled care of God's grace and are restored. In other words, the house will always be "Ralph's house" even though it will be more beautiful in its new and unfolding chapter.

The house had to be humbled, it had to be ripped and torn and demolished in order to become beautiful again, in order to be what it was designed to be. Failure is the stripping of boards, nails, and shingles, but love is the careful hand of a contractor who shepherds the house back to life.

What is being rebuilt in you? What is behind Jesus' question, in the moment of your failure, "Do you love me?"

QUESTIONS JOURNAL EXERCISE

Reinstatement

Revisiting our failures is not to be taken lightly. In this journal exercise the purpose is to revisit our failures in light of the love of Jesus that we see in the story of Peter and in our own lives.

If you are engaged in counseling for a deep and troubling emotional issue or situation, please talk with your counselor or spiritual director before engaging in this exercise. The discipline is not helpful if it is not healthy for your mind, body, and soul.

Take a moment to reflect on the story of Peter recorded in John 21:1-14. Imagine yourself in that boat, on that beach, listening in to every word of Peter and Jesus' conversation.

1. What failure would you bring with you to that beach? What loss, what misstep, or willfully destructive action would you carry into that conversation?

2. Jesus' three questions to Peter were "Do you love me?" Listen for a moment—what question is Jesus repeating to you? Write it down and sit with it for a bit.

3. What does this question mean to you at this point? What significance does Jesus' question have for you? How does he love you through this question?

4. Jesus ends each question by reinstating Peter—giving Peter back his purpose, and commissioning him for the work ahead. What would reinstatement look like for you in this moment of failure? What questions would you like to ask about the road of love that leads *out* of this failure?

CHAPTER EIGHT

a question of ritual

The work of God is carried out in the human heart.
In the ritual of reaching in and in the reaching out.
ROBERT FULGHUM

Why do we do what we do every day?

My wife recently experienced the "gift" of occupational downsizing. It was a gift in the sense that her job loss was an opening for us to enter into new, life-giving territory.

In calling this season a gift I don't believe that we're special in any way. I know folks who would be and have been deeply devastated by downsizing. We, for a variety of reasons, were ready.

My wife used this space to rethink her calling and for us to examine our family rituals and priorities. However, without the same demand on our hours and minutes every morning, we discovered a great gap in our lives.

We had lost our routine. We had greater freedom but had no idea what to do with it.

Daily life is often a beautiful dance between rituals that create boundaries and the freedom to choose those rituals in the first place. But what happens when our rituals lose their connection to our everyday life?

In our journey with Jesus, we find the same paradox. At times we need to stop and ask ourselves why we are continuing in certain spiritual practices. We live in rituals, routines, and disciplines only to have them lose taste and texture as we move from season to season.

What if rituals, routines, and disciplines hold the most important questions for our faith—the repetition of walking with Jesus? What might we find if we become courageously curious about the rituals, routines, and disciplines of the kingdom?

Washing Up

In Jesus' time, good Jewish people had a set of things to do when eating. These things weren't merely important, they were *divine*. Jesus and the disciples are sitting down to a meal, a huge event in a culture without fast food or Costco. The Pharisees, those who monitor the rituals, routines, and disciplines of Israel, come to Jesus with this question: "Why do your disciples break the tradition of the elders? They don't wash their hands before they eat!" (Matthew 15:2).

We all have table rituals. Some of us sit down and spray salt on basically everything. Some of us turn our plate a quarter turn to the right. Some of us turn, look at each other, and say, "How was your day?" Some of us aren't that warm. We eat quickly and in silence, either in fear of words exchanged or simply under the pressure of things yet to be done.

The Jewish people would wash their hands between every part of the meal, obviously for hygiene's sake but also to keep their minds on the subject of *purity*. One part of the Mishnah, a book of Jewish traditions that grew out of the written law of the Old Testament, is called *Yadayim* or "hands." It detailed the minute elements of washing your hands the way God desires.

The ritual, routine, and discipline of washing hands was important.

Life with God for the Jews (and for us as well) demanded a quality of purity and cleanliness, separation from things that were impure and dangerous. Washing was to separate life-giving hands from death-giving bacteria, symbolizing the separation of God's people from the darkness of death and self-destruction.

The process of providing clean water and clean utensils deepened the meaning of the ritual, giving beauty and depth to something very common and simple.

This ritual *defined* a people.

The Ritual of Birthdays

We do birthdays in our family. In other words, we *go big* when it comes to birthdays. We do balloons, cake, special dinners, surprise gifts, and multinight extravaganzas if they're feasible.

We shape that one particular day through a ritual, a routine, and a discipline in which we recall the past year and celebrate all the life and goodness that has come into our world because of that person. As a matter of fact, the rule is that as long as the balloons are still inflated it is still your birthday. One day just isn't enough.

Why? Because we're *alive*. Every year we have a moment to remember the year that's been, punctuated by the fact that we're still here and are probably better in one way or another than we were at the same time last year. Abraham Heschel says, "Just to *be* is a blessing, just to live is holy. The moment is the marvel."

Celebrating a birthday is a ritual and discipline that helps us attend to each other's lives and remember each other's sainthood—being set apart by God as good and having value beyond our imagination. Gordon Smith says, "When we meet a saint, we encounter beauty, integrity and congruence. The call to perfection is the invitation to be that for which we are created."

How we celebrate saints may change, but *that* we celebrate should not. The big picture is that we have a gift among us, the blessing of being, and it is a wise thing not to take that for granted.

The ritual of celebrating birthdays makes us the kind of people who celebrate life. The ritual of washing hands made the Jewish people the kind of people who lived into a special purpose, a special vocation. Rituals, routines, and disciplines are *creative* acts.

We engage in creative rituals every single day. We brush our teeth, not in any sort of religious way, but in a way that shapes and creates something in us. We sit in a quiet place (sometimes) and pray in order to learn what happens when we angrily, happily, anxiously, or sadly enter into a breathing space with God and get out of the realm of our own mental control.

Regardless of how or when we enter these spaces, it is always self-driven. It is always chosen. It erupts from our sense of *why* (see chap. 5). In a book about the daily routines of the most creative minds in history, Mason Currey says, "One's daily routine is also a choice, or a whole series of choices. In the right hands, it can be a finely calibrated mechanism for taking advantage of a range of limited resources: time (the most limited resource of all) as well as willpower, self-discipline, and optimism."

What if saints aren't born but are made, forged by the choice to step into a stream of creative rituals, habits, and traditions that seizes our limited life resources and through God's Spirit *re-creates* us over time?

When the Ritual Becomes the Point

The trouble with ritual, routine, and discipline is they can become the *point*. There is tension here, obviously. There are rituals that give us life and depth, and we don't want them to become a stepping stone to something else.

However, our rituals can become masters and not servants.

When Jesus engages with the Pharisees on the sabbath he says, "The Sabbath was made for man, not man for the Sabbath" (Mark 2:27). *Keeping* the sabbath had become the pinnacle of being, pulling a thick, dark curtain over the gold-glinted mystery of God, who cares for us and wants us to rest.

If we want to have healthy rituals, we have to come to terms with the reality that formation and transformation are not one-time things. Regarding sabbath rest, God intelligently and carefully gave his people a weekly (even an *annual*) practice. God didn't say, "Rest once a year, probably in the summer, and spend a grand sum on a place far from your home."

Instead, he says, "Six days you're going to work. Work is good. But the seventh belongs to me. Not because I need it but because you—my shifting and anxious people—need it. You need it weekly."

Sabbath reshapes the values of God's people. In effect, it says, *Work has an end, a limit. God is a great and generous Father, calming our hearts and bodies and souls. Every week we're reminded of this.*

The Jewish people would salivate at the seventh day, as the sun came to set on the sixth they felt the great burdens of work and worry shift off of their shoulders. They became a *people of rhythm.* They became saints, set-apart ones, pure and whole in a way that is distinct and different.

They were rested. They were trusting. They knew the safety of God's care. What would we give up to partake in sabbath if we realized *this* way of walking in the world is the real point?

When the ritual becomes the point, we are shaped for the ritual. When God is the point, the ritual shapes us for God. We are not slaves to the ritual, routine, or discipline. We can get so focused on the ritual and the discipline that it becomes a god—an idol. If we choose to break from that ritual or discipline, and move into another that shapes us for God, we can move with freedom.

Why do rituals and disciplines become idols? I believe it's because we can easily *control* them. We can check them off a list and gain some personal value and identity from doing it.

We can feel like we're moving the ball down the field in terms of our personal standing in the eyes of God. *I have done what I needed to do. I'm good for today.* Which rituals have become idols for you? How do you know?

Saints in Rehab

Is it possible that making peace with ritual and discipline requires me to make peace with the concept of religion?

In *Life's Too Short to Pretend You're Not Religious*, David Dark speaks of *religion* as anything we are "bound" to, tied up with, and deeply entwined in. If I think of other relationships (e.g., my marriage and family life) in which I am deeply entwined, there are rituals, routines, and disciplines that flow more or less effortlessly out of them.

We tend to put religion (strict structures and repressive regulations) on one side and relationship (free feelings and emotive expressions) on the other. When we look at Jesus, however, we see how rituals and relationships dance with each other.

We have somewhere forgotten that relationships always have a context, and the context for our relationship with Jesus is in fact *religion*.

Robert Fulghum relates religion to habits by calling it "a deep sense of connection through action with the unnamable wonder and mystery of life."

To have a relationship with someone is to engage in the rituals, routines, and disciplines that illustrate and illuminate that connection. From birth to birthdays, weddings and anniversaries, even as granular as daily conversation, we freely engage in the life of relationship. We are only free within those rituals and routines, however, if our great desire is the relationship itself. If not, we are slaughtering bulls and goats for no reason, trampling the courts of God like awkward strangers (see Isaiah 1:11-12).

Eugene Peterson says, "I cannot take charge of a ritual. I can only enter in—or not. Neither can I engage in a ritual by myself; others are involved. So a ritual, simply as ritual, prevents me from retaining any illusions that I am self-sufficient at the same time that it thrusts me into a life with others."

These rituals *root* us, deep down, in the good, clean flow of the God life. Psalm 1:3 says that those who savor the law of God are

> like a tree planted by streams of water,
>   which yields its fruit in season
> and whose leaf does not wither—
>   whatever they do prospers.

What would it look like for us to find the gift of rooting ourselves in rituals, routines, and disciplines that drive through the soil to the seeping water of God just below the surface of our seemingly mundane waking and walking?

In my early stages of faith, I somehow came to believe that keeping the rituals meant keeping in favor with God. If my day went south, I believed, it could be traced to my lack of morning devotions or my thinking too long about the girl who sat next to me in Spanish class. How did things ever get to that point?

I was given the rituals, covered with worn hands and under the prayers of old saints, but I began to see them as ways of earning favor instead of a way of becoming who I was created to be.

The Pharisees were the same; they got caught up in keeping score. They were invested and engaged in a system instead of the God who softly called out their names. Pharisees were not villains: they were simply completely consumed by the rituals and not the God who spoke them into being.

Being formed by walking with Jesus means being formed through ritual for the One who gave us life in the first place. What does that look like?

From Controlling to Creative

Jesus pulls back the curtain on what's really happening in the hearts of the Pharisees. They have turned to their traditions—their ways of keeping the law—instead of to the heart-moving laws themselves. In response to their hand-washing question, Jesus replied,

> And why do you break the command of God for the sake of your tradition? For God said, "Honor your father and mother" and "Anyone who curses their father or mother is to be put to death." But you say that if anyone declares that what might have been used to help their father or mother is "devoted to God," they are not to "honor their father or mother" with it. Thus you nullify the word of God for the sake of your tradition. (Matthew 15:3-6)

I need to pause here and notice that Jesus does not give an excuse for his disciples breaking with tradition. Apparently, the disciples were guilty as charged.

What if the tradition, the ritual, routine, and discipline, isn't nearly as important to Jesus as the reason for the tradition?

This is where curiosity is so helpful. When Jesus says, "Why do you sacrifice the heart of the law for the rituals of your ancestors?" he is inviting those of us who walk real paths in real skin to ask the question, Is this a wise ritual, routine, or discipline for my life right now?

What's the real value that God is forging in my heart and soul at this moment? Or, to turn the words in another direction, what am I missing in my life that I've replaced with a controllable, measurable ritual?

Jesus reveals what I see in my younger self, when I was engaged in the various gymnastics of obedience. When the ritual becomes the point, it allows us to skip out on other more important things that matter to the heart of God.

I wash my hands! So what if I skimp on my family? The *corban* law—declaring something to be "devoted to God"—allowed a person to dedicate their assets to a sacred cause rather than to their family. In a world where inheritance was survival, this was the ultimate act of manipulated holiness. This is for God; you fend for yourselves.

Similar stories today are so many that it causes my stomach to turn: a man attends church every Sunday, gives when the offering plate goes by, even leads a small group, but when he goes home he beats his wife and children. He hates, actively, those of another race. Something isn't clicking. He is not being formed into Christ through his rituals: he is simply walking paths that mimic the genuine and authentic spiritual life that comes when Jesus is at the center.

As I walk with people and teach them the Scriptures, two themes emerge when it comes to our perspective on the Bible's commands—*creativity* or *control*.

Just as a start, I believe many of our issues with God would be relieved if we saw the Bible as *creative* rather than *controlling*. Control is needed when there is chaos: violent crowds, a bleeding wound, and so forth are moments for *control*.

However, the great majority of our lives are not like this. In fact, if there's anything beautiful, anything good, anything lingering on this earth in the image of God, then creativity, not control, is the immediate need.

We can't speak good words to the world when we're bent on *control*. We aren't designed to *do* control well. When we're all about control, we don't have solutions to the world of chaos and conflict.

Our rituals and disciplines will be colored by whether we think God is more interested in creativity or control.

Is the command to love our neighbor a way of *making* humanity get along? Is the call to pray a way for God to ensure that we call home enough for his liking? Or with these directives does God have in mind some wise, deep logic that isn't necessarily concerned with the *how* of our rituals and disciplines but instead with the gift *within* them?

Creativity imagines a world where we're free enough to be with each other, to forgive whatever wrongs we've received, and to look to the needs of others rather than ourselves. To have this kind of creative and free interaction with God, we bind ourselves to the *wisdom* of the rituals and disciplines rather than the acts themselves.

I desperately need creativity in my rituals and disciplines. Tension is created when we live in a culture, even a culture of church leadership, where change for change's sake is assumed and even fostered. We have developed a skin-reddening spiritual allergy to doing the same thing over and over again.

On the other hand, I watch as my friends and I drink deeply of the liturgical calendar. We practice the daily office, we pray the psalms like urban monks moving from our cells and craving an inner stillness with God.

We saints, all of us, are looking for something: attending a Passover Seder, practicing mystic breath prayers, and bathing in the incense of another Christian tradition. What are we looking for?

The Wisdom of Clean Hands

Each law, each regulation, each piece of God's direction to his people—and in turn, each teaching of Jesus—is built to cut thick neural pathways in our minds that allow *wisdom* to flow continually.

Think about brushing your teeth. I don't know anyone who would say, "I'm excellent at brushing my teeth. I brush my teeth daily because I'm trying to get better at it. It's all about wrist angle, the amount of toothpaste, and the perfect follow-up spit. Here, let me show you my blog."

Brushing your teeth is an exercise that matters because wisdom says you don't want cavities, bad breath, or the sentence of a root canal.

What if the same applies to our walking with God? What if the whole point of sabbath is to teach us the wisdom of rest and relinquishment? What if prayer is good because it teaches us the wisdom of centering our mind and our will together with God? What if Advent and Lent are good because they wisely slow our madness to a crawl long enough for us to see the light of God and lament the death of God?

What if we could drink deep of the "wisdom of clean hands"?

When wisdom is the point, and we are free and creative with our rituals, a great field of exploration awaits us all. We may choose to step into the ancient traditions of the church, or we may choose to be personally and corporately creative and craft wise disciplines and rituals of our own.

Redemption of our rituals happens when the creative nature of the rituals, routines, and disciplines of our lives gives us wisdom and strength to walk with grace. The Pharisees, had they grasped the wisdom of clean hands, would have cared for their loved ones and let the hand-washing issue lie.

The dirty-handed Jesus stands before them, eyes softened with compassion, saying, "You have misplaced your values. Hope has already come. And his hands are dirty. Clean hands aren't the point—it's knowing the wisdom of the clean hands."

When the various laws and commandments were handed down, there was a note attached:

> In the future, when your son asks you, "What is the meaning of the stipulations, decrees and laws the Lord our God has commanded you?" tell him: "We were slaves of Pharaoh in Egypt, but the Lord brought us out of Egypt with a mighty hand. . . . [I]f we are careful to obey all this law before the Lord our God, as he has commanded us, that will be our righteousness." (Deuteronomy 6:20-21, 25)

God actually *expected* childlike curiosity, and it gave a chance to tell the bolder and more blessed story of Israel's rescue and renewal. Behind that, it provided a moment to say that the rituals and routines of the law were rooted in the identity of the recipients.

Without a playful, childlike curiosity about our rituals—without finding the wisdom of clean hands—what have we lost? What if we miss the gift in the ritual? What if we miss being rooted in the King and kingdom that make sense of the personal profanity and the litany of tragedy that we see each day?

Our rituals and disciplines, when we hold them to the light and in the right perspective, call us to search out *wisdom* and *creativity*, and to pay attention to the little and the less in our everyday, every month, and every year journey.

Fritos and the Body of Christ

A close college friend did three years in prison for some missteps strewn through his teenage years. He went behind the steel and ached, and in the midst of that valley he rediscovered the sweet and consuming presence of Jesus. Being a kid who grew up in church, he began to read the Bible again, but there was another longing within him: *communion.* Eucharist.

Obviously bread and wine were not options, but something sang in his soul when he thought about the elements, the spiritual food through literal textures, and so he did the best he could. Fritos and grape soda became, in symbol, the body and blood that sustained him through isolation and attacks on his identity.

Can saints really break bread with Fritos? To me, it is a question of whether we see the ritual and the discipline as the point or if we look beyond the ritual to the wisdom behind it. What is the wisdom of clean hands? What is the wisdom of breaking bread and pouring wine?

Why do I feel my soul opening in hope when I engage in a ritual so forceful as fasting or silence? Why do I constantly hear the echoes of the holy when walking a prayer labyrinth or engaging in sabbath? Is it possible that these rituals, routines, and disciplines are calling to the infant spark of sainthood within me, calling me to understand my birthright, the wise path set before me that calls me home?

Leighton Ford says, "In a very real sense we humans are spiritual amnesiacs, trying to remember who we are, where we came from, and where we must go to come home to our hearts."

In prison, in a living room, in kitchens and workplaces, wherever we are, is it possible that we aren't maintaining rituals in order to earn favor but to remember *who we are* and be attentive to *whose* we are?

Rituals and disciplines should draw us toward *attentiveness* not only to God but also ourselves and others. They should make space for natural, easy attentiveness to all the walking glories around us.

Leighton Ford describes attentiveness as "the very essence of our journey to the Center—as the way home to our own heart, the way of making our heart a home for God."

Spending time with our children, not just sitting in the same space but listening to the tales of the tiny worlds they inhabit and what they might fear going forward, is a forming and shaping ritual. We have to make time for that to happen, engage in it, and learn it well. It changes us.

Wordless walking with our spouse or significant other, even to simply hear them breathe, shapes us. We can't simply hope this happens; we have to shape our attention and time to allow for it. It shapes and deepens our relationships.

Engaging in corporate times of prayer, silence, and service helps us to surrender our personal cocoons and learn the wisdom of "loving one another."

Reading that book, the one that for whatever reason has grabbed our attention, shapes our minds, and therefore our life follows after.

Raking the leaves, mowing the grass, and cleaning the gutters are rituals that shape us into *something*.

If it is true that in him we "live and move and have our being" (Acts 17:28), couldn't the various rituals, routines, and disciplines of our lives become acts of repeated sainthood? But how would we know?

The Alternative to Sainthood

Living our sainthood, by design, is water and light instead of desert and darkness. It is life both to God who gives and to those around us who receive.

Jesus paints the alternative:

> You hypocrites! Isaiah was right when he prophesied about you:
> "These people honor me with their lips,
>   but their hearts are far from me.
> They worship me in vain;
>   their teachings are merely human rules."
>
> Jesus called the crowd to him and said, "Listen and understand. What goes into someone's mouth does not defile them, but what comes out of their mouth, that is what defiles them." (Matthew 15:7-11)

From Jesus' response, perhaps we could gauge our rituals, routines, and disciplines of sainthood by what they create? Washing our hands without caring for our parents, for example, creates pain and not life. In the words of Emil Brunner, "There is a devotion to God that hurts God because it hurts people."

Jesus names what I often see in myself when I have lost my rituals, routines, and disciplines. I find myself fighting to love well from a heart that is aching for wisdom. It aches to understand why it makes any sense to love someone who appears to be completely aligned against me.

It is chilling to think the one thing that could separate us from clearly seeing the mystery of the kingdom of God is the difference between engaging in rituals, routines, and disciplines, and knowing why it is wise to engage in them.

One of my great frustrations is that my own spiritual life isn't geared for that kind of wisdom. When we see through the ritual to the *heart* of the ritual, the loving and graceful One behind the ritual, we don't see through the eyes of unquestioning obedience but through the eyes of wisdom.

That is when God begins to mold and shape us, forming us into the saints we were made to be.

The Potter

Paul is a man in our congregation who does many things, but for solace and relaxation he creates pottery. He has a degree in ceramics, and all the tools of the trade are at his disposal.

With all the pottery metaphors in Scripture, I was curious about the process of making it.

I drove to Paul's house on a cold night, and inside he had cleared his dining room to set up the pottery wheel. He started by showing me how to knead the clay. The raw, dirt-scented thickness gave way under my palms. We worked out the air bubbles, each bubble threatening the finished product.

Once the clay was soft and flexible, Paul showed me how to center the clay on the wheel. Once centered, the clay would spin evenly and create something symmetrical and poetic in form. As I watched Paul, I noticed he seemed not to be *thinking*. Of course his brain was functioning, but his hands and mind were engaged on a subconscious level, repeating what they had known from thousands of hours at the wheel.

It was my turn. I sat at the wheel, my clay centered and my hands wet in order to keep the clay from sticking to my inept fingers. As I spun the clay, as my hands ran along the outside of the raw clay, I noticed that it moved. My fingers applied sturdy pressure, creating grooves in the clay. The grooves, the pressure, the lightness, and the firmness would create something over time.

The key was to apply consistent pressure. Paul coached me, "Press harder." Sometimes he would say, "Push right there. Move your finger there." He was speaking out of years of experience, knowing what each little pressure point would do to help create the final product.

What if the great Potter (Jeremiah 18:6) is giving us new opportunities today: rituals and disciplines, both new and old, which help our hands to find the work of beauty he has left for us in the world? What if repetitions that shape us at our core, giving light to our way, are waiting simply for us to discover them?

It is a question, I believe, worth asking over and over again.

QUESTIONS JOURNAL EXERCISE

Old Faithful

Rituals, habits, and disciplines aren't typically hotbeds of curiosity. If we aren't able to engage the core reason for our rituals, habits, and disciplines, they will always seem hollow and lifeless.

As you do this exercise, it may be good to take a few moments to think of the practical elements of your life that come to mind when you hear the words *ritual*, *habit*, and *discipline*. Write down whatever comes to mind. It is important to frame this journal exercise with some real-life examples.

1. Think about your faith tradition. What significant rituals does your faith community engage in? What meaning do those rituals have for you? What words come to mind as you think of these rituals?

2. Re-read the story of Jesus and the disciples discussing hand washing (Matthew 15). What rises up in you as you hear the accusations made of Jesus' disciples? What is the source of that feeling?

3. What are your current rituals, habits, and disciplines creating in your life? How do you know? What questions need to be asked about your current rituals, habits, and disciplines?

4. What wisdom might be available to you today if you engaged in specific rituals, habits, and disciplines? What might those specific habits and disciplines be?

CHAPTER NINE

a question of forgiveness

Forgiveness is the touchstone that distinguishes love from infatuation.

JOHN COWAN

How many times should I forgive?

My daughter had a habit that drove me insane. This may or may not make sense to you, but humor me for a moment.

She'd ask me, "Let me see your hand."

Then she would lick the back of my hand.

Yes I knew it was coming. Yes, I still gave her my hand. Being licked left that spit smell on my hand, that metallic smell that lingers because once I smell it the odor sticks in my nostrils. It's there for the day; I may as well get used to it.

That wasn't the problem with my daughter's habit, however. She asked again, "Let me see your hand." An argument ensued. I said, "No, you're just going to lick it again." We wagered back and forth, with her pleading, "I promise! I promise! Just let me see your hand." So I gave it to her.

Yes, indeed. She licked it again.

Questions of my sanity aside, as well as my daughter's fascination with licking people's hands, this is a fairly harmless lesson on what many of us go through daily in relationships. (As a side note, at the time of this writing it appears my daughter has grown out of the licking phase. Fingers crossed.)

We live with and around these beautiful saints-in-skin. If we're brave enough, we get into relationships with them. I say "brave" because we don't invest as deeply in each person.

There is risk.

There is uncertainty.

There is ambiguity about the motives and desires of others.

I invest in my daughter because she is the radiant combination of my and my wife's basic genetic framework. I invest in her because I want everything in the world for her. I want her to be well, holy, helpful, beautiful, and transformational in the world God has made. I'm invested. It is good.

There is another side to relationships, however.

There are those beautifully safe moments I experience with my wife, moments when I need forgiveness. Episodes and chapters in our lives when I have failed miserably, and then, coming like a convict to the judge's bench, I find softness, beauty, and embrace.

The offense could range from deep and cutting to merely irritating; it doesn't matter. I find safety with her, grace beyond what grace should be. And yet there it is.

Friendships blossom where together we hold deep and intimate secrets, confessions, and struggles. The yoke of life goes over two necks instead of one. We fulfill the law of love by carrying something that one person is incapable of carrying. There is great grace in this, because obviously our friends have a life of their own. They have a cosmos to manage, kids to feed and discipline, and an inner world to sweep and keep tidy. Yet they set it all aside and manage our mess with us. We return the favor.

There is something divine about that kind of friendship.

What if the entire reason for our relationships is our constant need for redemption? We thirst to be loved and belong, but we also need to be forgiven and learn to forgive. Kai Nilsen observes, "Jesus didn't come because all was well."

I hear stories of forgiveness. The release from mental and emotional prison for those who snatched deep and precious life from the world: murderers, adulterers, and abusers—all forgiven.

Others embrace and cultivate a minor slight for years until it becomes a beast that drags the hurt through all other relationships. How can one act be so powerful and the other so completely impossible?

Emotionally, spiritually, even physically, forgiveness should be a mystery to all of us. Shouldn't we all be incurably curious about the mystery of forgiveness?

What if the relationship we have with Jesus is driven by our deep need for redemption, to be forgiven and to be shown how to forgive? How do we learn the language of forgiveness and unconditional love without someone to teach us, to shepherd us through the process?

A Life of Forgiveness

Up to this point, we've talked at length about Peter. The apostle of grand statements and impulsiveness, Peter was unafraid of risk, even to the end. He said what was on his mind, and everyone else would have to live with it.

We have seen this behavior play out with goodness and holy revolution in Peter's life, and we also have seen it backfire. The question he asks in Matthew 18, then, sounds very curious indeed. "Then Peter came to Jesus and asked, 'Lord, how many times shall I forgive my brother or sister who sins against me? Up to seven times?'" (Matthew 18:21).

While standing on a mountain, Jesus' relationship with Peter, James, and John had recently entered a new stage as Jesus was changed into glowing energy right in front of their eyes. Moses and Elijah appeared, and a divine voice said, "This is my Son, whom I love; with him I am well pleased. Listen to him!" (Matthew 17:5).

I'd like to believe these three men, eyes widened to roughly the size of small dinner plates, were changed deeply. There's something within me that longs for that kind of experience, but at the same time I'd probably be looking for a flat spot to help build Peter's unnecessary shelters (see Matthew 17:4).

From there Jesus heals a possessed boy, predicts his death, gives a political stump speech on taxes, and then tells his disciples that if they want to be great in the kingdom of heaven, they have to occupy the lesser seat. You have to become childlike. I believe I've heard that one before.

Peter's question about forgiveness tumbles out at this point in the story. It's fascinating that Peter's whole life would be shaped by forgiveness, confrontation, suffering, and grace. I wonder if he knew how valid his question would be later on, after Jesus' ascension and the commission he and the other disciples would put into action.

Peter would call thousands to a life of change, stabbing into their hearts the reality that the long-awaited Messiah had come and they had executed him like a common criminal. *The one God sent, you have crucified. Let's talk about that* (Acts 2:37-40).

Peter's question about forgiveness is important for us. We walk with people who wound us. They tear holes in our souls, and when they see that bleeding reality they are broken in the deepest places. They feel guilt and shame, their eyes fall downward, and they look for our forgiveness. Though nothing can be the same, they enter into a softly lit space of grace, leaning on us to set them free.

Sometimes.

We also walk with people who have no grasp on the radiating circles caused by their actions or the way their words and movements wound us.

We typically enter into relationships unknowing, hopeful, risking our own energy and emotional health. And *those* are the men and women who raze us to the ground. It isn't as simple as saying, "They're evil people," which in fact may be true, but there is often more going on than we perceive.

The man whose father beat and demeaned him seeks to beat and demean others. What other way is there?

The person swaddled in the arms of addiction sees everything—people and resources—as nothing more than fuel for the fire of compulsions burning deep within.

The woman betrayed and jilted by a lover carries a steel plate over her heart and soul—sharing or cooperating are simply out of the question because history has a nasty habit of repeating itself. My money. My stuff. Look out for number one.

The son or daughter of the broken marriage, still limping through life while managing the cyclone of dysfunction that now affects their children and spouse, who are all new to the game.

These are the risks we all face in relationships, so how do we arrange our lives to respond?

Peter's curious question about forgiveness is a *shaping* question. He doesn't know it yet, but he is engaging in childlike curiosity and trying to understand what this new kingdom looks like.

So are we.

When Is Enough Enough?

Peter's curiosity opens the door to a question about forgiveness. When do we forgive enough? Well-meaning people say, "Jesus forgives us continually, so if we're his disciples, we should do the same, right?"

It feels excessive, like "How much love is enough?" or "How much ice cream is enough?" Clearly, the answer is "There's *never* enough."

Others say, "No, there is a limit. You can't be a doormat." An image of a weak Jesus pops up: grace is equated with *soft* or *weak*; forgiveness is heard as *compromise* or *giving in*. Jesus the forgiver becomes Jesus the frail flower in a field of chaos.

Neal Plantinga speaks of this chaotic world as the "vandalism of shalom." Forgiveness is the active repair and restoration of the peace of the world. It does not occur top-down, by some sort of organizational policy, but relationally, one to another spiraling up and up in a glorious ascent. This is not weakness but emotional and spiritual exertion at the highest level.

What is the alternative? Self-protection or cynicism, or even worse.

We have internal conversations where we tear our enemies down, with every razor-sharp blow approved and motivated by a sense of God's approval.

They're against you.

They need tough love.

They need to hit bottom; maybe this will help.

It's true, there are addicts who need their families to host an intervention and drive them to rehab. There are abusive spouses who need to feel the chill of coming home to a quiet house instead of a set of moving targets. There are manipulative, draining people in our lives who steal every last minute of our time and every last bit of our energy if we don't wave the white flag and invite them to a discussion about boundaries and expectations. These are possibilities, however, not *probabilities*.

My struggle is that I find it easy to confirm each possibility. I too easily use words like *rock bottom, codependent, unhealthy relationship*, or even *abusive*. While these are helpful, they are also distracting.

In one of the most moving moments in the movie *Forrest Gump*, Jenny returns to the house where she was abused as a child. She stares down the weather-beaten and abandoned house, and then throws rocks at the windows with all the emotional force of a wounded child rising up in rage at all that has gone before.

She crumples, weeping, and we're led to think this is some sort of cathartic moment. There is nothing else said on the matter. To the viewer, it is a beautiful moment of reckoning with pain and the past. It is that, but we can't get lost in the fact that it isn't forgiveness. It isn't the kind of letting go that gives hope and heart to all of us, even the abused and wronged among us. It isn't restoration of shalom.

So how does forgiveness, real and genuine release, restore shalom?

Honestly, I don't think Jesus would agree with our definition of forgiveness. That's why I believe we find forgiveness so difficult. We aren't shaped for the grace it takes to engage in the process of forgiveness. So, what shapes us?

Forgiveness on Display

In response to Peter's question, Jesus dives into a story often called the parable of the unmerciful servant. The title isn't really helpful, because the quality we see on display in this story, which Jesus crafted specifically to help Peter through the forgiveness question, is far from simple mercy.

Mercy is stepping back from crushing someone else. Mercy is what happens in some baseball leagues when a team is getting beaten 13-0 and has no chance of coming back: the game is called. That isn't what is happening in this passage.

Throughout Jesus' story, the Greek word *splagchnizomai* is used, which is translated "mercy" or "compassion." This word literally means "to be moved in the bowels or innards."

It is the word that describes my emotion when I see children who have been sold into sex slavery, when infants are brutally murdered, and when children live in abject poverty and play in overflowing sewers.

It means "to feel it in our guts," but even more so to have cleared space in our guts to feel it.

In response to Peter's question, Jesus says that a king was settling debts, and a man came to him owing ten thousand bags of gold

(Matthew 18:23-35). He had borrowed this gold, which rightfully belonged to the king, and he was obviously trying to duck out on the payments. One bag of gold (talent) equaled about twenty years of wages for such a day laborer. The king ordered that the man and his whole family be sold—sold into slavery, in a sense—until the debt is paid back.

This is a place of deep darkness, for the debt won't be paid back any time soon. The man is in over his head, and technically it's his own fault.

The worker begged the master "Be patient with me and I will pay back everything" (v. 26). Again, the questions of *how* and *when* and *why* come to our minds. If he *could* pay it back, why hasn't it happened already? He's way behind.

"The servant's master *took pity* [*splagchnizomai*] on him, canceled the debt and let him go" (v. 27).

A thought occurs here: What impact does this forgiveness have on the master? It cost him something. The reality of suffering with someone as we forgive them, to really know them well enough to be compassionate, even when we're the one offended: forgiveness always begins with the other first.

To Suffer With

Over the years, I've tried to embrace what Scripture says about the things that change us as people. The life and teachings of Jesus point to one particular thing as the transformational catalyst toward becoming the best version of ourselves.

It's typical of all workout programs.

It's typical of all diets.

It's typical of all healthy and growing relationships.

It's typically something we avoid like the plague.

If we want to find the thing that tips the scales, that draws us into new light and deeply roots us in who Jesus is and who we're made to be, then we are called to *hurt.* We are called to suffer, because it is what those we want to walk away from are constantly *avoiding.*

Suffering is the banner of Jesus, who is truth walking with people, and suffering is a part of living in such a way that we're connected deeply both to our world and the people in it. Suffering is horrible. Suffering is something we pray against, pray about, and pray through, and yet it makes more of us than we have categories to understand.

Suffering requires the presence of *compassion,* which Frederick Buechner defines as "that fatal capacity for feeling what it is like to live inside somebody else's skin. It is the knowledge that there can never really be any peace and joy for me until there is peace and joy finally for you too."

It's hard to tell why Peter asked Jesus about forgiveness, but it makes sense to me that Peter may have been *hurting.* If he's like us, he bears deep wounds. He has people who have broken him, wounded him, and left him stranded by the road.

What if forgiveness is suffering, paradoxically, with the person who caused our suffering?

Jesus responds to Peter's question: "I tell you, not seven times, but seventy-seven times" (Matthew 18:22). Imagine how tedious, how life-sucking it would be to keep track of how many times you forgive one person. Imagine keeping a spreadsheet with dates, offenses, and the conclusion.

May 5: dude cut me off in traffic, made an obscene gesture—forgiven, 5:25 p.m. after a day of work and a few conversations in my head.

Could it be that the tediousness is Jesus' point? Is the playful side of Jesus coming out? "Well, Peter, the answer is exactly seventy-seven times. Give that a try. Next?"

You could keep that list of offenses, but apparently you only have to have seventy-seven entries, or 490, depending on what translation you read. At that point, what do you do? Is there a point where you stop forgiving, really?

Honestly, this is a significant question for those of us who are curiously chasing Jesus, truth in skin, on the issue of grace and forgiveness. What does it look like to truly cut someone out of the stream of forgiveness, toss them to the fates, refuse to be human to them or with them, and refuse to let yourself think of their redemption?

The great mystery is that if we cut someone off in this way, we're the only ones who move. We step away from them, we remove ourselves from relationship, and we step into a place of constant and continual punishment of them in our heads.

Sounds beautifully appealing, doesn't it?

What happens to our souls? To our hearts and our motivations? We're constantly dodging what we might feel about them, the recurring memories of whatever fond conversations we may have had. We might feel a sense of guilt because this is part of following Jesus, but at the same time we can't go back *there*. It's just too painful, too much work, and no one expects us to put up with that kind of thing, do they?

When we have been hurt and wounded, there's a point when the path of forgiveness feels like we have a ripping headache while sprinting through a hall of funhouse mirrors: *at some point, this has to release*. When our wounds come from family or friends, forgiveness feels like a daily habit of revisiting both the pain and tormentor just as we have the day before.

Lather. Rinse. Repeat.

Forgiveness that is deep enough to suffer with another person will always expand, not end, the situation and circumstances we're facing. This flinty kind of compassion allows us to forgive, but *never* forget.

Instead, suffering with someone we're forgiving helps us remember differently. When we walk this path, what kind of character and life are formed in us?

Is it possible that forgiveness rises and falls on our ability to consider others (Philippians 2:3)? What if we fail to suffer with someone on the journey of forgiveness because, frankly, we can't consider them important at all?

In the words of David Augsburger, "Forgiveness refuses superiority."

Jesus' teaching here is deliberate. The master of the story *felt with* his servant. He put himself in the servant's shoes and saw the servant's wife and children as his own. He felt deeply what it must have been like to be saddled with this tremendous debt that was never going away.

I have felt the burden of the debt: when I was in need of forgiveness, when I had charged like a bull and shattered everyone around me with reckless abandon. I felt like I had left a trail of bodies, a trail of victims. I knew I was in the darkness, hands covered in blood, as guilty as the brightness of summer sun.

Forgiveness Gives Thanks

I have also been *owed* by debtors: my life given in loan to others and then trampled, misused, unused, and cast aside. I've had trust violated and leveraged into selfish adventures that benefitted no one but the adventurers themselves, either at my expense or the expense of my family and other friends. Nonetheless, I am grateful.

Without gratitude, forgiveness is impossible. Without a sense of what we've been given—the sheer grace of God—forgiveness will be a futile exercise. Gratitude gives forgiveness shape, color, and depth.

Gratitude and forgiveness round out our lives, in a sense. But Jesus is also shaping us *against* them. They batter us, gently shaping us like pebbles on a creek bed constantly pressed by the weight of the water. Jesus is injecting grace into the world, calling us to curious explorations such as "how many times should we forgive?"

To chase the kind of forgiveness that shapes us requires us to become vessels that hold the kind of grace we need to release others from their debt on a regular basis.

What if we are conduits of forgiveness, holding loosely what has been given to us because it doesn't belong to us anyway? We're formed to live as if giving forgiveness is intertwined with receiving it. In Emily Freeman's gifted image we are "colanders of glory water," pouring out that which Jesus has poured on us.

Refusing forgiveness also shapes us. We ache with the loss of relationships. We feel our soul's capacity shrink because we lose the infusion of grace that it takes to push against the firm edges of our lives. Joy becomes difficult. We see every new person as being like our offender, and we treat them as such.

In my life, few things need the incarnate Jesus more than my own approach to forgiveness.

The Opposite of Forgiveness

In a strange turn, Jesus' story continues. The man who had his debt forgiven by the king finds someone who owes him one hundred silver coins, which was equal to a little more than three months' wages. The former debtor demands repayment. He refuses pity, compassion, or mercy, and has the man and his family thrown into prison (Matthew 18:28-30).

We can get carried away reading this story as if it actually happened. It didn't. Jesus artfully created an impossibly wide gap between the first debtor and the second in order to make a point.

The king hears about the lack of forgiveness and acts swiftly. The first debtor is given back his bill and then is tortured until he pays it back (Matthew 18:32-34).

I wonder whether at this point Peter wished he hadn't asked. Remember, the question at the beginning put him in the position of *forgiver*. I don't know if Peter had a reason, a situation in mind, but now he had to wrestle with a large and imposing reality.

To the degree we have been forgiven, we learn to forgive. To the degree we have been shown *compassion*, we should show compassion, to feel what it's like to be the one who has wounded you, with all the darkness and denial.

The root of the Hebrew word often translated "forgive" literally means "to bear," "to lift up," or "to carry away." When engaged in the trench work of forgiveness, we long for our injustices to be "carried away," but we often are immersed in "bearing" and "lifting up" the load of our wounds. Forgiveness, either way, is a weight to be carried.

What does this tell us about the kind of soul—the kind of will and desire—that is cultivated for forgiveness?

Again, the incarnate Jesus—God in the flesh—helps tremendously here. He knows how it feels to be wounded deeply, to be in the position as the forgiver, and so he feels for us when we are in that place as well.

We in turn can feel with those who are in *need* of forgiveness, who come to us (or not) with a debt. In their eyes we see ourselves.

We see ourselves broken, foolish, embarrassed, and guilty. We see the way we avoid or justify our actions, the way we try to rationalize the waves of pain we've set free with our actions. We see it. We know it. We feel it. Forgiveness is a statement that we know the far-off country from which those who have wounded us have come.

I don't find this to be easy. In the relationships where forgiveness takes time, where it seems to be a battle, it is very hard to see any beauty. When we feel our pain so acutely that we can't possibly get around the pain, it is easier to stay where we are.

We don't move *away* from forgiveness, but we don't move toward it either. We keep it at a distance, quietly watching from behind thick glass and hoping someday we can "do it."

Here we need to encounter a brutal question about forgiveness.

Our Life's Work

What if forgiveness takes a lifetime, and perhaps beyond?

The moment I knew I wasn't supposed to work with teenagers anymore was when I began to listen to their issues and think, *In about three years, the thing that you're struggling with isn't going to matter at all.* When we're growing and developing, which is whenever we're still breathing, it is hard to get the big picture, the long view of life.

Forgiveness, in the story of the unmerciful servant, is all about the long view. We'll struggle with forgiveness if we can't see beyond the offense at hand. We'll struggle with forgiveness if we believe that it is an even exchange.

Finding the long view of life when it comes to forgiveness begs us to ask the question, and the question beyond the question. Forgiveness starves without curiosity, becoming childlike enough to know that we can't see the long view, and we need to ask questions beyond just the wound at hand.

While I was writing this chapter I had a chance to talk with Matthew Soerens, who works with World Relief, an agency that resettles refugees in the United States in a safe and legal way.

Prior to knowing better we both thought immigration was a matter of the right paperwork and the right process. Wrong!

Instead, even a person who has family in the United States and a job waiting can wait up to fifteen years to get through the process. Think of it: a teenage son living in the United States would enter midlife before living in the same house with his father or mother. His childhood would be gone before he could sit at the same table. It is painful, and reform needs to happen.

The truth about forgiveness is very similar to immigration. Too many of us see forgiveness as a matter of *paperwork*: We say the right words. We give the right permissions. We have the right feelings. We become naturalized citizens of the land of the "forgivers."

Wrong!

Forgiveness isn't an exchange. It isn't one and done. It really isn't even "forgive and forget," because one part of that equation is wise and the other is not. You forgive the dog, a beast by nature, for snapping at your hand. But you don't put your hand back down for a second try.

Jesus' teaching, carried through by his disciples, is simply to *forgive*.

One of the reasons curiosity is so important to our growth and formation is that it's not enough to hear Jesus teaching "forgive," and then we *do* it.

We need the second question—the curious question—*How?*

When it comes to forgiveness, the *how* is not just an event. It's not just an action, an attitude, a prayer, or a gift given in hopes of burying a hatchet.

Forgiveness is an address. It's a place where you live.

We have a sense that at some point we will walk too far with our friend's trust; we will inadvertently trample the emotion of our spouse or significant other; or we will disappoint a parent or trusted mentor in a very personal way.

Forgiveness is a *thing* because my ability to wound and betray are things. Forgiveness is a *thing* because redemption and restoration are things I can't live without.

We are always accompanied by others. They are constantly present, shaping us as we strike against them or lean on them.

We'll need to forgive and be forgiven, but again, how?

When we answer the *how* of forgiveness, we answer it with our whole lives. Forgiveness is a state of being—both forgiven and forgiving—and to enter it is a permanent revolution of the soul.

When Jesus says, "Unless you forgive your brother or sister from your heart," your Father won't forgive you, he isn't describing an exchange. This isn't a matter of paperwork. He's inviting us to a way of living, becoming a conduit that receives and gives away, that welcomes and sends, that builds a house on the borders of redemption, burns the U-Haul, and lives in the middle of constant renewal and release of those who've wounded us.

Forgiveness isn't about paperwork. It's about *presence*. It is the way we walk in the world, never to return again. To do anything else is to die as a refugee, a person without a holy country, who is in search of life.

The question is, Where, who, and what are we fleeing? Where would we rather live?

How many times should we forgive?

QUESTIONS JOURNAL EXERCISE

Letting Go

Forgiveness is a space of great risk and vulnerability, but also a space of great joy and possibility. We want to treat this journal exercise with a high level of grace and gentleness, knowing that for everything that needs to be forgiven, there is a wound deep enough to kill our spirit.

This journal exercise will be a bit different from the others. The point of this exercise is to help us engage the process of forgiveness with a deep and penetrating curiosity. The end result will be sharing our curiosity with those who have wronged us or are in need of our forgiveness. You may not be capable of that yet, but I pray you'll allow God to shape you into the kind of person who might forgive as you have been forgiven.

Spend some quiet time before you begin this journal exercise. Pay attention especially to the feelings in your body as you consider this exercise. Where do you feel tension, uneasiness, or irritation? Embrace that feeling as a real and genuine outcome of what's going on in your heart and mind.

1. Recall the hurt or issue that came to mind when you were reading this chapter. Hold it before God, and without making excuses

acknowledge why it has wounded you so deeply. What do you feel as you bring this before God? What is familiar about this conversation? Why?

2. What questions still haunt you about this wound or event? What questions would you like to ask the person who wounded you?

3. What thoughts do you imagine were going through the mind of the person who wounded you when they acted in the way they did? What might God be saying to you about their motivation or role in the event?

4. Think about forgiveness as an act of compassion toward the person who wounded you. What does that mean in your particular situation? What questions do you need to ask Jesus when it comes to being compassionate toward the person who has wounded you?

a question of change

The mystery always contains more mysteries. Do I really want it this way?

ANN VOSKAMP

What are you talking about as you walk along the way?

As we come and go, we greet each other with some variation of the question, How are you? or What's up? If we're being transparent, we know that sometimes we say this to be polite, but sometimes we ask because we're concerned or curious about that person's spot in the cosmos at that moment.

Casual acquaintances respond with "I'm fine" or "Nothing." Deep friendships respond with detail, frustration, joy, and ambiguity. Perhaps "What's up" is a bigger question than we think.

Picture two men walking along the road and Jesus asking them, "What are you discussing together as you walk along?" (Luke 24:17).

There is likely no more normal, ground-level question than to ask people what they're thinking about. It is a request for access to their simple, everyday life, a request to hear the echoes and whispers that have made up their conscious hours thus far. Our curiosity runs head-first into practicality.

Curiosity matters only if we are attentive to real life.

Henri Nouwen observes, "The spiritual life is not a life before, after, or beyond our everyday existence. No, the spiritual life can only be real when it is lived in the midst of the pains and joys of the here and now."

Pains and joys.

Here and now.

These contexts and containers of the spiritual life are built to brim with curiosity.

The great grace of curiosity is that it allows us to enter difficult and unsteady rooms of life and find the centering, peaceful presence of Jesus inviting us to come deeper still. This is how we live joyfully, hopefully, even though we feel a mortal wound (Job 13:15). This allows us to sing "Amen" to Julian of Norwich's statement of resilience: "All shall be well, and all shall be well, and all manner of things shall be well."

However, even as I write these lines I know the pain of people who don't find all is well. Those of us who have sojourned in the wild of "trying harder" and "letting go and letting God" only to find ourselves exhausted, guilt-ridden, and painted as joyless. If we are doing it right, we should feel alive—not dying—shouldn't we?

Yet that is where we are. Things are changing, and it's killing us.

The tension and the guilt, as we know, create a moment for curiosity. As we craft this discipline of letting our questions rise unfiltered, perhaps we will find a way through.

Is there a way to move through change, loss, and pain with our souls intact? What tools, guidance, or insights on how to journey joyfully through change do we find in Jesus?

What if, in fact, dying is not only the point, but it is truly the way to live?

A Map for the Journey

One quiet sabbath I was reading and happened on a concept that stopped my eyes. In his book *The Holy Longing*, Ronald Rolheiser paints with bright and engaging colors the idea that the spiritual life follows the pattern of *crucifixion, resurrection,* and *ascension.*

All of my life these words have been deeply holy, cascading off the shoulders of Jesus. I know he challenges us to "take up [our] cross and follow" (Matthew 16:24), but it is difficult to imagine my own crucifixion. However, the thought of resurrection and ascension are welcomed with open arms.

But what if the passion (the death, resurrection, and ascension of Jesus) is actually the model for how we find joy in the rolling changes of life?

What does crucifixion look like for the successful business owner, coming to the age of retirement and packing up the corner office?

What does resurrection look like for the single mom dented and drawn out from long work and longsuffering separation from her children?

What does ascension look like for the thirty-three-year-old widow leaving the cemetery that's shrinking in the rearview mirror?

Could we possibly find hope in embracing these movements of Jesus' passion in our spiritual lives? Whether we like it or not, we find ourselves in this process even now.

Finding Our Way

We have more access to information now than perhaps at any time in history. I recently asked my wife to check the weather on her phone, even though my laptop was in my hand, because her app was faster. This actually happened.

Apparently, I don't have time to waste on typing and clicking.

In his book *Nonsense,* Jamie Holmes says, "We're all drowning in information, a reality that makes even the simplest decisions—where to eat, which health plan to sign up for, which coffee to buy—more fraught." Does access to information mean we end up making the right conclusions, choices, and assumptions?

My wife and I were flying back to the United States from the Caribbean, and our connection back to Chicago went through Miami. Since it was an international flight, the greatest challenge came when we had to pick up our checked bags and recheck them for our flight back to Chicago. To accomplish this Herculean feat, we had to find our way from the international terminal to the connecting baggage claim in the basement of the airport. There were stairs and escalators, but very few signs.

Thankfully we stayed close to others who were making the same connection, or else we may never have found our bags. We might still be in Miami, for all I know.

What we were missing is called *wayfinding*. Wayfinding is the art of moving people, clearly and obviously, from one place to another. In places such as airports, theme parks, and hospitals, wayfinding is essential. Why? Wayfinding is essential because without it, we're left with ambiguity.

We can handle only so much ambiguity. The space between signs, between points of information and direction, has to be short so we know we're headed in the right direction.

What signs are we currently following in our faith and formation?

In my own journey, I have found information about Jesus helpful. I have found good direction for my journey by studying the life of Jesus and all the people who have written new ways to turn his beautiful prism so that new light shines through.

But when I rise early, put the coffee on, and begin to meditate on the day to come, I don't need more information about Jesus. Honestly, I need some secret goodness that I can practice in my words and work. I need to know him in a way that motivates, guides, and restricts me.

I need to know, as Dallas Willard says, how to "do what Jesus would do if He had my life."

I need direction.

John says that anyone who wants to walk in the light must walk as Jesus walked (1 John 1:7). The root of this "walk" idea is the Jewish concept of *Haggadah*. It is a way of living and conducting oneself in the world based on who we believe God is and where we believe he is guiding us.

Jesus' life is a living Haggadah, wayfinding, in other words. It is a script that welcomes curious improvisation as we enter into situations and circumstances with no parallel in the historical life of Jesus. Times have changed in our changing world.

What happens, however, when change brings death? Can we find hope in Jesus' journey through death as well?

A Long, Hard Walk

In Luke 24, we see two men walking away from Jerusalem. Their heads hang, lolling left and right as they move through the eclipsing daylight spattered through the trees along the road. They are headed toward Emmaus, a small town where they have a place to stay and collect their thoughts. A great deal has happened recently, and they are overwhelmed (Luke 24:13-14).

The men are leaving Jerusalem on the third day after the tragedy of Jesus' death. The day when Peter and John had seen an angel, when the women had mistaken Jesus for the gardener, and perhaps when they themselves had seen the empty tomb.

But *they* hadn't seen Jesus. Some of the women in their company reported something amazing. Jesus had made good on his word, rising from the dead three days after dying a violent death at the hands of the brutal Romans. The men were not convinced.

The two men believe their wondrous work in the world is apparently over, and they are beginning to sort through both the realities and their expectations. Everything has changed. All their expectations have been frustrated.

I want to grant the disciples some grace here. The two walking toward Emmaus are struggling with reality, and rightly so. Death had happened. People don't come back from crucifixion. That's reality. They had heard repeatedly the accounts of Jesus' destruction, and the mental pictures played on an endless loop.

Resurrection was still a rumor. Crucifixion was the only certainty.

In my own life, I've seen this to be true as well. The jobs I dreamed about early on drifted quietly away, and in their place were disappointment and the temptation to become cynical. Later, a new dream took their place, equal in majesty and exceedingly more beautiful and rich.

At the time, however, all I could see was crucifixion. Death. Disappointment. How do we look backward and reflect on the light that came out of darkness while looking forward and seeing only darkness in the future? I believe crucifixion, resurrection, and ascension are the three key moves we need to keep in mind as we walk through change.

Move 1: Crucifixion

For something to come to life, something else has to die.

Whether we ask for it or it comes unbidden, death is a reality of our everyday world. It is our companion. Including crucifixion as a companion in our journey is painful, but not unrealistic. We feel things die. We see dreams, hopes, and expectations fall deeply into the earth. We who live and walk with Jesus know that part of the death we experience is the death of deadly things, the choking off of the things that draw our souls down into death (see Colossians 3:5-11).

It at least makes sense to surrender those destructive things, though we have to confront and admit our secret comfort with these dark streaks in our souls.

But what about the death we don't choose?

We can't bring ourselves to understand *or* embrace the crucifixion that steals our light and causes sleep to steer clear of our eyes. It causes spiritual insomnia, causing us to walk the floors in the depths of darkness, praying for the process to reverse itself.

As I write this chapter, a school bus moves down our street. On any given day it holds small units of grace who are entering into a relationally complicated world. Maybe one comes from a divided home. Perhaps his dad has moved on to other places and people. The gap left, specifically for a young boy, leaves him searching for answers to the changes in his body and his way of seeing himself in relationship to other boys.

An abusive home leaves children walking on one foot, so to speak, imbalanced and unsure of themselves because they have learned that they are not worth care and concern. They are a rag doll tossed about on a sea of systemic and cyclical brokenness well beyond their control.

An indifferent home leaves a child aching for attention, negative or otherwise, to quench their thirst for connection to others. They feel like an afterthought, an addition, a secondary character in a great drama who is left to go it alone.

I watch the bus roll by, with the small heads barely showing above the windowpanes, and I am both joyful and fearful for them. They are either joyful or fearful themselves. Life for them is difficult, punctuated with moments of joy, and they walk it with more courage than we will ever know. How do they walk in the world with these stories hanging heavy on their shoulders?

They walk like the men from Emmaus.

They are walking in the way of *crucifixion*.

They walk with death every day.

What does it look like to walk daily with death? How do we learn to be okay with death?

Holding Things Loosely

The most recent joys of my life have come as I've learned how to hold things loosely. My wife and I have tried to practice simplicity in everything we do, but specifically with our possessions. We look for things that are necessities, and keep a few things that give us joy, but beyond that we are very familiar with our local thrift store. We had to crucify something in ourselves, however. The cultural mandate to possess, just in case, was so strong that it took a while for us to engage deeply in this practice.

Curiosity is what drove us there. Simply asking "Why do we still have this?" is enough to bring to light our motivations and drives. Am I keeping that charcoal set because I don't want to acknowledge that I never formed the discipline to use it? Am I keeping that shirt because I hope to wear it someday?

This seems like a gentle form of dying, but it can be a dress rehearsal for the larger relinquishments we're asked to do throughout our journey. Sometimes we have to kill off our attachment to things. Sometimes we have to crucify our expectations for our lives, our children and spouses, and even possibly our Messiah and leader.

In the Bible the word *deny* is sometimes translated "disown." For example, Jesus tells Peter that before the rooster cries three times "you will *disown* me" (Matthew 26:34).

For those of us who want to cultivate curiosity, practicing the discipline of asking beautiful questions on the journey of our faith, we will at some point have to enter into mystery and remain there. We will need to disown one thing, and stand empty-handed for a while. These are our little deaths, our little crucifixions.

Certainly, there is pain in crucifixion. The reason many men and women suffer through midlife transition is because we lack the grammar of healthy death, of proper and necessary crucifixion.

Our friends on the road to Emmaus are walking in the light of *crucifixion*.

Loss.

Confusion.

Uncertainty.

The paradox of our whole life with God is this: when we are most open, willing, and fertile for curious engagement with God (and our own soul), we struggle to find our way to the light. We are overcome by our linear map of the world being shredded and thrown to the wind. You can see this gap, this aching struggle when these grieving disciples sum up the whole story of Jesus in the phrase "we had hoped . . ." (Luke 24:21).

I wonder if the beginning of curiosity in our own crucifixion comes when we can bravely say, "We had hoped . . ." (fill in the blank).

What would you and I have to *repent* of—literally, change our minds about—to embrace our particular moment of crucifixion?

The Crucifix and the Empty Cross

At a recent silent retreat, we gathered in the chapel of a Jesuit retreat center. My eyes were drawn immediately to the images nearly flying off the walls of the chapel. Our retreat leader began pointing out the different paintings and wall hangings, and then he came to the crucifix.

Serving in an evangelical Christian context, we display the empty cross. Our church serves many who grew up in the Catholic faith, so we get the question "Why is your cross different?" on a regular basis. I had always explained the cross on our wall as symbolizing the resurrection, that Jesus is no longer there. The empty cross is a sign of victory.

Then the retreat leader called me to repent. A little.

As he described that very same difference—the crucifix and the empty cross—and said profoundly that the gift of the crucifix is that a suffering, bodily Jesus is something we can identify with.

We know how to suffer.

We know our bodies feel pain.

We know how to bleed, weep, and in some sense how to die.

This thought arose in my soul: *in the journey of our lives, we need both the crucifix and the empty cross.* We *identify* with the crucifix, but the empty cross *inspires* us. The tension of our lives is that while crucifixion is pervasive, unstoppable pain, without it there can be no joy in the empty and bare cross.

The men from Emmaus are so blinded from the idea that there could be an empty cross that the Scripture says when Jesus came near "they were kept from recognizing him" (Luke 24:16).

What if the very thing that *keeps*—literally "arrests"—the minds of the men from recognizing Jesus is that they *only* identify with crucifixion? What if it's actually easier to imagine dying than rising? In the midst of crucifixion, Jesus draws their minds to examine reality. *What are you talking about?* They respond, shocked that this man hasn't heard.

> [Jesus] was a prophet, powerful in word and deed before God and all the people. The chief priests and our rulers handed him over to be sentenced to death, and they crucified him; but we had hoped that he was the one who was going to redeem Israel. And what is more, it is the third day since all this took place. In addition, some of our women amazed us. They went to the tomb early this morning but didn't find his body. They came and told us that they had seen a vision of angels, who said he was alive. Then some of our companions went to the tomb and found it just as the women had said, but they did not see Jesus. (Luke 24:19-24)

Is it possible that in asking what they were talking about, Jesus was helping the men *process* the death of their expectations?

When we bravely map crucifixion over our own lives, seeing how light has a place to break through the bleak boundaries of our pain, we begin to imagine how crucifixion can *become* something.

Ronald Rolheiser calls this the difference between *terminal death* and *paschal death*. He says, "Terminal death is a death that ends life and ends possibilities. Paschal death, like terminal death, is real. However, paschal death is a death that, while ending one kind of life, opens the person undergoing it to receive a deeper and richer form of life."

What questions are swimming around in the sediment-heavy waters of our current season of crucifixion? Is there life in it? What does this death bring to life?

It is here we see the second movement—*resurrection.*

Move 2: Resurrection

When we begin to map the *paschal cycle* onto our own lives, things begin to rise to the surface. In fact, this moment between crucifixion (in the minds of the two men) and resurrection (Jesus' presence with them) is a pivot. Julie Barrios says, "A pivot occurs when a limitation gives birth to a potential creative possibility that would never have been considered otherwise." For Barrios, this is part of a larger formation process that consists of "orientation, disorientation, and reorientation." We are alive. We wander, lost, in death. We are reacquainted with life through resurrection.

Jesus' question and response to the men from Emmaus inspires a pivot: *Tell me how you're dying, and I'll tell you where you'll live.* In other words, everyone suffers crucifixions of one sort or another, but in Jesus' story crucifixion always leads to resurrection.

The person we planned to spend the rest of our lives with dies of cancer, but there is life yet to come.

The job we thought we'd retire from is eliminated, but there is life yet to come.

The energy and body we thought was inexhaustible begins to slow down, break down, and fail, yet there is life still to come.

Jesus corrects the men from the perspective of the one who went through death and has seen the passageway through the darkness.

It had to be this way.

Crucifixion is important because it *limits* us, reminds us that we are not eternal. The limit creates a possibility: we become humble, grateful, content, and realistic. These are the songs of a new life, and we learn to sing them.

What if the greatest movement in the disciples' (and our) formation is learning how to respond when our expectations are nailed to the cross only to be resurrected in a new and living form?

What if most of our questions help us to engage with our defied expectations, our grand disappointments, and our unseen detours by walking the path of crucifixion and resurrection with Jesus?

Jesus says in John, "Unless a kernel of wheat falls to the ground and dies, it remains only a single seed; but if it dies, it produces many seeds" (John 12:24). In other words, "in order to come to fuller life and spirit we must constantly be letting go of the present life and spirit."

For resurrection to come, there must be crucifixion. What good can come from that?

Jesus is talking about glory. Resurrection is the glory that comes after death finally dies. "Did not the Messiah have to suffer these things and then enter his glory?" (Luke 24:26). If we want to see glory, goodness in full light and strength, it appears that the path runs through the cross.

Is this God's design for the world? What if, as we follow Jesus through the dark of crucifixions both great and small, we find glory smiling on the other side of the darkness? How would we know?

Death and Life by Design

In its aging and maturing the human body daily goes through cellular death and resurrection to ascend and live.

Steve Hayner was president of Columbia Seminary when he was diagnosed with pancreatic cancer. A brilliant and vibrant man, Hayner and his wife, Sharol, recorded their thoughts and struggles on the CaringBridge website, which is for those suffering with major health crises. Their blogs are recorded in the book *Joy in the Journey*. As I read it, one thought engaged me deeply regarding the paschal kind of spirituality: "Grace can never be learned once and for all. It must be explored through each new circumstance. It must be experienced, received, and savored. It defies scrutiny but requires reflection."

Though Steve did not survive his battle with cancer, he received grace upon grace as he was crucified, resurrected, and ascended—never to be the same.

Is this cycle simply for tragic and fatal crucifixions? Or are there little deaths that mirror this cycle as well? What if grace isn't simply a happy gift but is also the fruit of learning how to die well?

Human relationships go through the crucifixion of the first fight, the resurrection of forgiveness and reconciliation, and the ascension of a new way of being with each other.

I know that one day I will have to crucify my role as a father whose child needs me. I will have to crucify my status as a young leader with "potential" and become whatever my ordered steps have led me to be. I will one day have to crucify my assumption that my body will do the things it has done in the past, letting others lift for me instead of feeling the resistance of weight against my hands and knees. However, there are new gifts to be found—glory even—in the resurrection that comes in later years.

The paschal cycle that Jesus went through and the men from Emmaus struggled with is actually the way all of life works. Jesus walked that path, that Haggadah, so that we might live through it differently.

What will my life look like at that point? I can't scrutinize it, as Hayner says. Scrutiny leads to regret and living in death, which clouds our ability to see resurrection with the full light and beauty Jesus evokes.

But what happens *after* we see the beauty of resurrection?

Move 3: Ascension

When I had pneumonia several years ago, my body went into power-saver mode and I hit the couch with a dull thud. Though I didn't quite have the feeling of crucifixion, burial seems like an adequate image. I wallowed in deep sickness for a few days, ingesting enough orange juice to keep citrus farmers everywhere smiling. After rest and medication I found myself free to breathe and walk as I used to. My mind and body went briefly to a place of wondering, *Man, what was it like not to be sick?* But then I came out on the other side to rediscover myself.

I wasn't the same, however. Now, I don't handle cold weather quite as well. My lungs seem to remember what happened so many years ago and begin to protest with the first subzero breath. I'll never be the same. What does that mean going forward?

It has always intrigued me that Jesus appeared to Thomas in a resurrected body that bore scars. Like a brand-new model with dings in the hood, Jesus' hands and side were reminders.

These things really happened, yes.

Resurrection really happened, yes.

However, nothing is the same.

How can God be God when I'm not the same? How can my life be deeply engaged with Jesus when so much of what I now take for granted has been crucified through time, challenge, or circumstances? Life is different. I am different. What happens now?

This is called *ascension*. Rising, beautiful and strong, and never going back to the way things were before. What does that look like?

The two men and Jesus arrive in Emmaus, and the men ask their curious companion to stay. It is getting late and the sun's disappearance cued criminals and malcontents to take the stage.

They invite Jesus to their table. I try to remember that this is a hideout, a "bunker." Those closest to Jesus have kept a low profile these last three days, unsure of what fate awaits them once Jesus' charisma no longer covers them.

They may be trembling—they likely have few resources and even fewer prospects. It is indeed a bunker, a place of hiding from darkness and death.

We've all been in that bunker before, where we are being shaped by adversity but are also struggling to see the light of God in the middle of all that is against us. Like King David, we feel the weight and cry out "save me from my enemies" (Psalm 18:48).

We struggle to keep our eyes clear, looking upward from and attempting to hold every circumstance to "the inner light."

Now in the midst of their questions and ambiguity, this stranger, Jesus, is with them in their hideout. They trust at a time when nothing seems trustworthy. They care deeply, loving as Jesus had taught them (Matthew 22:38-39). He must have been beaming, even as they were downcast.

Jesus was, despite their inability to see it, present in their moment of crucifixion. He was present because he had been through crucifixion and resurrection and could usher them into the next place: *ascension*.

What would it mean, in the midst of the questions we've kindled through reading this book, for us to suddenly realize we have someone walking with us? What if we came to know that a calming, beautiful presence was at our side on the road?

Would the intensity of our need for answers relent? Would our breathing slow and our minds relax?

They offered hospitality. He broke and blessed the bread. "Then their eyes were opened and they recognized him, and he disappeared from their sight" (Luke 24:31). They recognized Jesus in these symbols of his humanity. The bread he broke and the table where they gathered were common symbols, and Jesus used them for a completely different reason.

The men on the road to Emmaus were made aware of who this curious man was by familiar symbols—bread, table, and presence—but then they were drawn to reflection. "Were not our hearts burning within us while he talked with us?" (Luke 24:32).

Is it possible that in the midst of our confusion, our pain, and our drama Jesus actually came and walked with us? As Phil Yancey says, when we were most curious and disoriented, "God did not give us words or theories on the problem of pain. God gave us himself." Jesus' presence guides and directs through curiosity.

Through the ritual of breaking bread, we see he is with us.

Through our failure and slowness to believe, he is a loving presence along the road.

Through the moment when we have lost our identity and have been named among the criminals and scoundrels, he calls us "those who God dines with."

Through the moments when we wrestle with being wounded, wondering what it might look like to set a place at the table for our enemies, he carries the forks and knives, and sets each place with grace.

What would it look like to order our lives around Jesus, who is with us through all the terror and glory of change? That is an excellent question.

QUESTIONS JOURNAL EXERCISE

Learning to Die

The final chapter is likely the heaviest of the entire book, comprising the weighty issues of death, resurrection, and living new life. At this point you undoubtedly are at one place on the paschal cycle. You may be going through a period of crucifixion, where things are dying either by your own choice, the choice of others, or simply as a product of your life stage.

You may be in-between stages as well—moving from old dead stuff to new life or moving into new life and realizing nothing can be the same. Let the questions exercise here help give depth and context to your journey, wherever you find yourself on the cycle.

1. Take a moment and think about what you felt as you read this chapter. What questions still remain after your reading? Write them down as quickly as they come to mind.

2. Listen as Jesus asks you, "What are you discussing together as you walk along?" (Luke 24:17). What would you need to ask yourself or others in order to understand what you've been living through lately?

3. What are your biggest questions regarding the crucifixion going on in your life? Don't be afraid to write what is bubbling up in your spirit.

4. What are you curious about in the resurrection that you see in your life right now? What questions do you need to ask about this new life?

5. What kinds of questions come to mind when you think of ascension—that nothing can be the same again?

6. What is the dominant question you're taking away from this book and the journals? What new questions might God be bringing to mind right now?

conclusion

FINAL QUESTION

There are no events but thoughts and the heart's hard
turning, the heart's slow learning where to love and whom.
The rest is merely gossip, and tales for other times.

ANNIE DILLARD

Jesus says, "I am the way and the truth and the life" (John 14:6). This passage is typically part of the way Christians do battle against other religions. We strip that passage of all goodness, however, if it is only a word on who is right and who is wrong.

What does that really mean? What does it mean for Jesus to be the way, truth, and life?

Jesus says, "I am the truth." If the truth is a fact, statement, or detail, then we simply need to memorize it and move on. It is what it is. St. Nicholas of Serbia says, "Truth is not a thought, not a word, not a relationship between things, not a law. Truth is a Person."

Yet Jesus is a *person*. The Word—God's speaking in action—is a human being, a person who can't be memorized, can't be reduced to a statement or a fact, but instead longs to be *known*. Curiosity is the richest sense we can cultivate in learning to know the truth-in-person that is Jesus.

We walk winding paths and are changed by the experience. We act and react based on the world we live in. Knowing people, knowing a person, means we know them in a variety of situations, challenges, and circumstances.

The curious tension of Jesus is that he shows us a God who wants to be *known*, not memorized. Paul talks about his goal for people being to "know the mystery of God, namely, Christ" (Colossians 2:2).

What do we do with truth that lives, breathes, and walks with us—the mystery of God in the flesh, dancing with the common glory of those made in the image of that very God? How can we not become curious?

The process of getting to know someone relationally gets derailed when we are both too busy to stop and listen, and convinced that knowing *about* someone is the same as *knowing someone*.

Our souls and spirits ache to know the truth, not just the details. And to know truth, we need better questions. My hope is that this book has equipped you with reflections and insights that help you curiously chase this truth, this Jesus.

Knowing the Truth who loved good food and fine wine.

Knowing the Truth who answered hard questions with questions.

Knowing the Truth who lost loved ones, was betrayed by those close to him, and in the end experienced one of the greatest perversions of criminal justice the world has ever known.

Knowing the Truth who said, "What can I do for you?"

What do we do with the Truth who both walked in an ancient world not so distant from ours and walks with us in our present world?

Can we entertain the thought that this tension is actually the great grace of God in full bloom? Is it possible that he loves us too much to give us too much certainty? Does he move like a tender parent, closing the container of cookies, knowing that the point of "too much" is rapidly approaching?

To be sure, when the goodness of God meets skin and bone, we are going to find more questions than we can possibly ever answer.

To be shaped in curiosity, to be shaped and formed in our spirits, means we have to engage the question, *What does it look like to walk the path of transformation with our whole being, our whole self needing attention and formation?*

If the truth is a *person*, if the road we must walk is a *person*, if ultimate reality is a *person*, then doesn't it make sense that we get to know that person with as much speed and intensity as possible?

I believe that the way to know Jesus is to learn to ask curious questions, as many questions as possible, in every changing moment and situation.

Know that questions are welcome.

Know that you are not alone in asking.

Know that our first questions are only scratching the rich and beautiful surface.

Jesus is calling us to become curious. Will we answer?

acknowledgments

I couldn't have managed something like this on my own.

This book is the fruit of many people—some who prayed, some who edited, some who provided encouragement or guidance or space or time for these ideas to come to light and life in a way that made sense.

Thanks to Caleb Kaltenbach for giving me the energy and encouragement to even start the project and bring what was once in darkness out into the light.

Thanks to Don Gates and The Gates Group for helping promote the manuscript and get it through the processes necessary for publishing. Thank you for being a wise guide.

Thanks to Cindy Bunch, Jeff Crosby, and the team at IVP for their work in editing and promoting and encouraging me in the writing process. It was work in community, and I appreciate your heart for writers and writing, and the deeper shaping of God.

Thanks to the folks who read the early versions of the manuscript: Nikki Fontanetta, Jennifer Johnson, J. K. Jones, Colleen Bente (thanks Mom!), Trevor Hinz, John Robinson from Lightstream (Australia), and the Eastview Spiritual Formation group. Your feedback was instructive, corrective, and ultimately a blessing.

I also want to thank those at Parkview Christian Church who have encouraged me and asked numerous questions about the book and when it was going to be done. Thanks especially to Bill Brown, Tim Harlow, and Dan Leverence for giving me the space to do the work.

Many voices have come out in various ways in this book—writers, teachers, preachers, and professors—who have shaped this book immensely: James Bryan Smith, Dallas Willard, Rick Ryding, Henri Nouwen, and Neal Windham. Thank you for helping honor my curious questions.

Thanks to my friends who helped put energy into everything from the intricacies of the writing life to the social media end of things: Ian DiOrio, Arron Chambers, Michael Kimpan, and Rick Champ. Thanks for helping to get the word out!

Most importantly, thanks to Holley and the B—my biggest inspirations and cheerleaders—who have given up time with me, surrendered my attention when writing needed to be done, and celebrated harder than anyone else when things clicked and began to flow. Thank you both so much. I love you.

leader's notes

This guide is for church and faith-community leaders who want to help others (and themselves) understand and engage in the spiritual practice of asking questions. The questions and information here will help you and your friends on the journey to ask those childlike questions throughout the course of life.

Don't feel as if you have to go through every chapter's exercise, but instead choose relevant chapters for you and your community.

The following are the most helpful things for you to do as a leader:

1. *Prepare.* You should read the chapter and the questions ahead of time, making sure you have an idea of where the discussion might be headed based on the content for that meeting.

2. *Allow for extra time.* The subject matter of this book is built to elicit questions, so leave time for people to have silence (even awkward silence!) to process and share questions that might come up as you talk together.

3. *Protect each other.* Becoming curious is a spiritual practice that isn't always readily accepted. People in your group may decide to risk a "crazy" question. Don't look at them as if they just set fire to the rug. Instead, receive the question and help them process why that question is important to them.

4. *Share.* I would love to hear about your questions, experiences, and challenges, so please don't hesitate to connect with me via Twitter (@cktygrett) or contact me through my website www.caseytygrett.com.

Blessings as you lead, and I pray that your discussions and processing will be fruitful not only to the individuals in your group but to the group as a whole.

Introduction

The introduction is designed to open up the line of thinking that *curiosity matters in the life of faith*. Spend some time thinking about your own experiences or your current level of curiosity when it comes to your life with God. It's important that as you guide others you understand where you are walking or have walked in the past.

1. In the introduction we find the quote from Seth Godin that says learning to be curious is "more about a five-, ten-, or fifteen-year process where you start finding your voice, and finally you begin to realize that the safest thing you do feels risky and the riskiest thing you can do is play it safe." How does this quote strike you?

   Does it relate to a relationship with God or not?

   As a group, make a list of both positives and negatives that strike you as you read the quote.

2. Where do you find examples of curiosity in the Bible?

   What stories, teachings, or events reveal how God works through curiosity?

3. The author hopes to give us three gifts through the book: the gift of permission, the gift of tension, and the gift of rest. Which gift appeals to you most?

   Which gifts feel like they are at odds with becoming curious?

4. Take a moment to read Matthew 11:28-30 aloud, preferably from *The Message* translation of the Bible. Have the group close their eyes and listen to the reading. Read it as many as three times, and

ask group members to think about questions that come to mind from the text.

After the readings, ask the group to share their questions. You don't have to answer the questions; just let them be. Write them down and keep them somewhere where you can return to them as a group later in the study.

As you leave your group time, encourage everyone to read chapter one and do the Questions Journal Exercise at the end of the chapter.

Chapter 1: Why Curiosity Matters

It would be good for everyone to come into your time both having read chapter one and Matthew 3. The Matthew text will help to center the discussion.

1. Discuss any quotes, thoughts, or questions that came to mind as you read this chapter.

2. At the beginning of the chapter the author says, "I wonder if sometimes doubt—doubt that troubles the faithful and even disconnects people from a journey of faith—is simply curiosity cast as a villain?" What experiences have you had in the past with doubt?

   How does it feel to think that doubt actually may be something productive, like curiosity, made to seem like a *bad* thing (i.e., a villain)?

3. The author talks about Jesus' first words, "Repent, for the kingdom of heaven has come near" (Matthew 3:2). What impressions did the discussion on *repent* make on you?

4. How have you heard the word *repent* used in the past?

   What new questions does the chapter raise for you going forward?

5. How does it affect you to know that Jesus interacted with around 183 questions in the Gospels?

As a group, what are your favorite questions by or asked of Jesus? (Some of these questions may be addressed in future chapters of the book!)

The author says, "if we cannot safely ask new and curious questions with him, then we have to wonder if Jesus is sufficient to address the reality of being human and being alive." What do you think about this statement?

Whether you agree or disagree, explain *why* you feel that way.

6. How did the exercise at the end of the chapter feel for you?

What was helpful, what was confusing, and what was difficult about the practice?

As you leave your group time, encourage everyone to read chapter two and do the Questions Journal Exercise at the end of the chapter.

Chapter 2: Growing Young

At the beginning of your time together, consider watching the intriguing TED talk "Returning Curiosity in Schools: Un-silo-ing Education" by Laura Akesson (https://www.youtube.com/watch ?v=M1064-tMOJU) to set up the discussion for the night.

1. What thoughts, challenges, or questions do you have after reading chapter two?

At this point, how do you find your responses changing to the readings?

2. Have you ever considered activities such as play to be spiritual? Why or why not?

3. What challenges you most about the idea that engaging in spiritual practices is an act of childlike trust that God is going to take care of you, even when you're fasting?

4. Talk about a time when you asked a question that made you feel vulnerable.

How did that situation turn out and what did you learn from it?

What new questions came from that experience?

5. Read Matthew 18:3-4. Do you agree that Jesus' call to become like a little child means we should return to asking curious questions? Explain.

6. The author says, "The harder we try to remain in our certainty of adulthood we end up looking like the worst version of our childhood selves: spoiled, protective, and filled with suspicion that everyone wants to take what's 'ours.'" How do you think we can keep our childlikeness and still do all of the adult things we have to do?

7. With all the talk about childhood and the author's own experiences from childhood, what emotions are stirring in you?

What new questions do you need to ask about your own childhood and how God might be using those memories to teach and form you today?

As you leave your group time, encourage everyone to read chapter three and do the Questions Journal Exercise at the end of the chapter.

Chapter 3: What Do You Want Me to Do for You?

Entering this session, it would be good to reflect on the journal exercises from chapter two. Childhood memories can be beautiful, but they can also be painful. It might help your group to have some time to process them.

1. What insights or questions came up as a result of reading chapter three?

2. Have you ever looked at the stories of James, John, and Bartimaeus in this light? Why or why not?

3. As a group, go back and re-read Mark 10:35-40 together. As you read, imagine yourself in the place of one of the three main characters. What comes to mind?

4. Are you uncomfortable with Jesus asking you "What do you want me to do for you?" Why?

   Would you know how to answer that question if he did?

5. The author says, "Curiosity may invite us into risk and tension, but it can also readjust the way we see reality. That's what it means to be a 'learner'—a disciple—of Jesus." How have you found this to be true in your own life?

   What question would you love Jesus to answer right now?

6. What do you make of the idea that Jesus may fulfill your request and you may then enter into a very normal life, like Bartimaeus?

As you leave your group time, encourage everyone to read chapter four and do the Questions Journal Exercise at the end of the chapter.

Chapter 4: A Question of Identity

As the beginning of this session, have the group listen to the classic song "Who Are You?" by The Who. Lyrics are available online, and you can find the song through any streaming music service or on YouTube. Not only will you help some unfamiliar folks hear a classic band, the song sets up the discussion well.

1. What questions or challenges come to mind after reading chapter four?

2. How do you relate to the idea that life is constantly pressing us to identify ourselves, to say and prove who we are?

What happens to our faith if we give in to that constant pressure?

3. The author says, "The discipline of curiosity allows us to not only see ourselves for who we really are but also to repent of believing we will never be anything more than that." How do you react to this quote?

How might curiosity help you understand who you are in your current stage of life?

4. The author makes a tie between identity and the Lord's Supper. How do the bread and wine (or juice) help you to remember who you really are?

5. What is the story behind the reason your parents gave you the name you have?

How do you think your name has changed the course of your life?

What name do you believe Jesus would give you if he were here right now?

6. Give everyone a small piece of paper or an index card and ask them to prayerfully consider the harmful, false, destructive name they've been given by other people. Have them write that name down and put the cards in a bowl or container. If you feel comfortable, burn those cards as a symbolic way of saying, "Jesus renames me every day."

As you leave your group time, encourage everyone to read chapter five and do the Questions Journal Exercise at the end of the chapter.

Chapter 5: A Question of Motivation

A good opening to this section would be to ask a silly question such as, What breakfast cereal best describes you, and why? With this week's discussion of motivation, this will help the group see what matters most or at least what's most consistent with who they are and why they do what they do.

1. What thoughts, questions, or insights came to mind while reading chapter five?

2. Read through Jesus' encounter with the expert in the law found in Luke 10:25-37. After reading this story and spending some time in silence, what part of the conversation sticks in your mind? Why?

   What part can't you stop thinking about? Why?

3. What do you think about the idea that law creates both tension and beauty?

   What beauty can you see in law?

   How is God present in that beauty?

4. Which question—*what*, *why*, or *how*—is easiest for you to think about? Do you think it's easier to take a "Just do it because I said so" approach or a "This is why and how you do it" approach? Why?

5. How has the Internet affected your curiosity?

   What things don't you remember anymore because you can simply look them up?

   What impact do you feel this has on a life of faith?

6. What do you make of the fact that many of Jesus' teachings have answered the *what* and *why* questions but leave the *how* questions up to us?

What would happen if God actually trusted us to partner with his Spirit and carry out the *how* in our own little worlds?

As you leave your group time, encourage everyone to read chapter six and do the Questions Journal Exercise at the end of the chapter.

Chapter 6: A Question of Others

In preparation for this section I recommend that you spend some time in a public place such as a mall, an airport, or a train station. As people walk by, make a note of what makes them *different* from you (e.g., appearance, ethnicity, gender, even religious traditions if it's obvious). Thinking about differences will prepare you to lead this discussion well.

1. What thoughts, questions, or challenges came up while reading chapter six?

2. How would you answer the question, Who is your neighbor?

   Describe the person that came to mind when you read Luke 10:29-37.

3. Put yourself in Jesus' audience, listening to the story about the good Samaritan. How would you have responded to the story if instead of "Samaritan" Jesus had said the name of a group you despise, oppose, or suspect of having evil intentions? (Identify that group in your head and keep it with you as you hear Samaritan.)

4. The author says, "chaos is part of walking with God." Do you agree or disagree? Why?

5. How have you avoided loving your neighbor because of the suspicion that loving them will be messy?

   How does God's love for your messiness challenge you in this discussion?

6. Thinking about loving your neighbor—either the name you came up with in question 3 or simply someone in your life—what would you have to risk in order to love that person well?

What would you stand to lose in loving them?

As you leave your group time, encourage everyone to read chapter seven and do the Questions Journal Exercise at the end of the chapter.

Chapter 7: A Question of Love and Failure

The content in this section could be difficult for the group. This may be a good time to reiterate the need for confidentiality and sensitivity to the stories being told within the group. If you feel comfortable, be prepared to tell your story of failure first so that others feel comfortable sharing theirs as well.

1. What thoughts, insights, or questions came up as you read chapter seven?

2. Read John 21 as a group. Where do you find yourself in that story?

What kind of tension do you feel as you think about how Peter reacted to each event in this story?

3. The author talks about having to apologize to his daughter. When have you had to admit that you failed someone?

What did you receive as a result of that conversation?

How did you change as a result?

4. The author says, "In my moments of failure I have found Jesus to be far less spectacular than he is kind and common." What does this mean to you?

Is this a comforting idea, a challenging idea, or something else altogether different?

5. If, as it appears in the Peter story, Jesus is inviting us to participate in our own comeback from failure, how does that change the way we see forgiveness and restoration?

What changes as we accept that invitation?

6. What might God want to do with your story of failure?

How might he be inviting you to take your experience of failure and use it to help others who have experienced the same thing?

What is the first, easiest, and most obvious step you need to take to use your story of restoration?

As you leave your group time, encourage everyone to read chapter eight and do the Questions Journal Exercise at the end of the chapter.

Chapter 8: A Question of Ritual

As you begin, ask the question, What was your favorite family tradition growing up? Consider texting this question to your group ahead of time, and have them bring an item to your group meeting that reminds them of that family tradition.

1. What insights, challenges, or questions came to mind as you read chapter eight?

2. What is one daily routine that, if you lost it, would completely ruin your day?

3. The author says, "Rituals, routines, and disciplines are *creative* acts." Do you agree? Explain.

What have your rituals and routines created for you and your family?

4. This chapter discusses sabbath rest as a meaningful ritual or routine. What place does sabbath have in your life?

If it has no place, why is that?

5. Talk about a time when you witnessed a situation where someone did all the good "Christian" rituals but showed that their life wasn't being changed.

When has that scenario described your own life?

6. How does describing good rituals and routines as "wise" help you understand the difference between something rote and boring and something life-giving and joyful?

7. How did the description of the potter at the end of the chapter connect with your own experience of the rituals in your life?

What kind of vessel has God shaped your life into through your rituals and routines?

As you leave your group time, encourage everyone to read chapter nine and do the Questions Journal Exercise at the end of the chapter.

Chapter 9: A Question of Forgiveness

As in chapter seven, the content in this section could be emotionally and spiritually sensitive. Have the group begin with prayer and remind them that this group is a safe place for all stories and discussions that might come up.

1. What questions, insights, and thoughts came to mind as you read this chapter?

2. When you talk about forgiveness, what is the first thing that comes to mind?

Why do you believe that particular thought pops up?

What might God be teaching you through that thought?

3. Do you see forgiveness and grace as signs of weakness or strength? Why?

4. The author says, "Honestly, I don't think Jesus would agree with our definition of forgiveness. That's why I believe we find forgiveness so difficult. We aren't shaped for the grace it takes to engage in the process of forgiveness." Do you agree? Why?

How would you define *forgiveness*?

5. How does embracing suffering help us understand how forgiveness works?

How can we start taking a more active approach toward embracing forgiveness in our lives?

6. The author says, "Forgiveness is an address. It's a place where you live." How does this description change the way you see forgiveness in your own life?

As you leave your group time, encourage everyone to read chapter ten and do the Questions Journal Exercise at the end of the chapter.

Chapter 10: A Question of Change

The final chapter is one that will hopefully leave you with more questions than answers, as well as a path forward on the way to becoming curious. Leave some time in this session to talk with your group about what they've learned and what questions are still left on the table as you end this series.

1. What are some questions, challenges, or insights you came to while reading this chapter?

2. The author says, "Curiosity matters only if we are attentive to real life." How does that thought strike you?

How have you seen this to be true in your life?

3. Recount a season of change in your life when you found people, thoughts, or events that served as wayfinding, helping you find your way.

4. Read the account of the two men on the way to Emmaus (Luke 24:13-32). What do you feel when the men respond to the "stranger's" questions?

   How would you have responded if you were in their place?

5. Look at the three key moves of change—crucifixion, resurrection, and ascension. At this point in your life, which move do you find yourself in the midst of?

   What does that experience feel like to you?

   How is God teaching you through that movement of change?

6. As you close your time, have everyone share their most critical question at this time in their life, the gnawing question that they would like God to answer at this stage.

Conclude your time by praying for each other's moves in the journey of change and that curiosity would be a constant companion for them going forward.

notes

Introduction

9 *more about a five-, ten- or fifteen-year process*: Seth Godin, *Tribes: We Need You to Lead Us* (New York: Portfolio, 2008), 64.

God is the same yesterday, today and forever: Michael Hidalgo, *Changing Faith: Questions, Doubts and Choices About an Unchanging God* (Downers Grove, IL: InterVarsity Press, 2015), 14.

12 *Tension means*: "Tension," *Wiktionary*, accessed October 17, 2016, https://en.wiktionary.org/wiki/tension.

1 Why Curiosity Matters

23 *That's the bewildering side of forty*: Peter Greer and Greg Lafferty, *40/40 Vision: Clarifying Your Mission in Midlife* (Downers Grove, IL: InterVarsity Press, 2015), 28.

26 *God I know*: Aaron Niequist and his team are leading an ambitious worship community called the Practice, held at Willow Creek Community Church (www.practicetribe.com). You can find their music and liturgies at www.anewliturgy.com. This particular song lyric is from liturgy 5, "Here Are My Hands."

the Dunning-Kruger effect: Sarah Lewis, *The Rise: Creativity, the Gift of Failure, and the Search for Mastery* (New York: Simon & Schuster, 2015), 24.

27 *A soul will never grow*: John of the Cross, quoted in *The Complete Guide to Christian Quotations* (Uhrichsville, OH: Barbour, 2011), 243.

28 *Ignatian Examen*: A great resource on this is the original text of Ignatius of Loyola's *Spiritual Exercises*. For a more contemporary take, see *A New Liturgy* website, featuring teaching by Fr. Michael Sparaough on the examen (www.anewliturgy.com/06.html).

2 Growing Young

30 *It is a beautiful thing*: Johann Christoph Arnold, *Endangered: Your Child in a Hostile World* (Rifton, NY: Plough, 2011), 20.

Childhood means not having to commit: Ian Leslie, *Curiosity: The Desire to Know and Why Your Future Depends on It* (New York: Basic Books, 2015), 22.

31 *around four years old*: Susan Engel, quoted in ibid., 31.

32 *He had to learn how to drive*: Tom Smith, *Raw Spirituality: The Rhythms of the Jesus Life* (Downers Grove, IL: InterVarsity Press, 2014), 33.

33 *Nobody is more needy*: Larry Crabb, *Shattered Dreams: God's Unexpected Path to Joy* (Colorado Springs: WaterBrook, 2010), 17.

3 What Do You Want Me to Do for You?

45 *He is bread to the hungry*: John Flavel, quoted in *The Complete Guide to Christian Quotations*, 245.

48 *downward mobility*: This thought occurs throughout the book by Henri Nouwen, *In the Name of Jesus: Reflections on Christian Leadership* (New York: Crossroad, 1992).

51 *The Gospel of Jesus Christ*: Jen Pollock Michel, *Teach Us to Want: Longing, Ambition, and the Life of Faith* (Downers Grove, IL: InterVarsity Press, 2014), 29.

4 A Question of Identity

67 *We need to see how often*: Parker Palmer, *A Hidden Wholeness: The Journey Toward an Undivided Life* (San Francisco: Jossey-Bass, 2009), 34.

69   *Identity and value are found*: Robert Mulholland, *Invitation to a Journey: A Roadmap for Spiritual Formation* (Downers Grove, IL: InterVarsity Press, 1993), 89.

70   *I cannot give*: Palmer, *Hidden Wholeness*, 83.

5 A Question of Motivation

78   *By supplying answers to questions*: Ben Greenman, "Online Curiosity Killer," *New York Times Magazine*, September 16, 2010, www.nytimes.com/2010/09/19/magazine/19lives-t.html.

80   *A fundamentalist is*: Seth Godin, *Tribes: We Need You to Lead Us* (New York: Portfolio, 2008), 61.

84   *does not present us with a moral code*: Eugene Peterson, quoted in Barry Jones, *Dwell: Life with God for the World* (Downers Grove, IL: InterVarsity Press, 2014), 31-32.

     He who is within us: Thomas Kelly, *A Testament of Devotion* (New York: HarperOne, 1996), 6.

85   *When a company*: Simon Sinek, *Start with Why: How Great Leaders Inspire Everyone to Take Action* (London: Portfolio, 2011), 53.

86   *Whatever I decided*: Barbara Brown Taylor, *An Altar in the World: A Geography of Faith* (New York: HarperOne, 2010), 50.

6 A Question of Others

94   *Knowing your neighbor*: In Jay Pathak and Dave Runyon's book *The Art of Neighboring* (Grand Rapids: Baker, 2012), they provide a helpful chart, which can be downloaded here (www.artofneighboring.com/wp-content/uploads/2016/01/blockmap-1.pdf). The beginning, they say, is to actually identify your neighbors—the people who literally live beside, across from, or behind you.

95   *fear is the enemy*: Elizabeth Gilbert, "Choosing Curiosity over Fear," in *On Being with Krista Tippett* (podcast), July 7, 2016, www.onbeing.org/programs/elizabeth-gilbert-choosing-curiosity-over-fear.

96   *We will continue to despise*: Jean Vanier, "The Wisdom of Tenderness,"
     On Being with Krista Tippett (podcast), December 24, 2009, www
     .onbeing.org/programs/jean-vanier-wisdom-tenderness-3. This is Vanier's
     paraphrase of thinking he attributes to Dr. Martin Luther King Jr.

     If you want to know the condition of your heart: Bob Goff, keynote ad-
     dress, North American Christian Convention, Anaheim, CA, July
     13-15, 2016.

7 A Question of Love and Failure

106 *Jesus asked [Peter]*: David Benner, *The Gift of Being Yourself: The Sacred
     Call to Self-Discovery*, expanded ed. (Downers Grove, IL: InterVarsity
     Press, 2015), 30.

     It began to occur to me: Carl Rogers, *On Becoming a Person: A Therapist's
     View of Psychotherapy* (New York: Mariner Books, 1995), 12.

108 *This King, full of mercy*: Brother Lawrence, *The Practice of the Presence
     of God* (New York: Cosimo, 2006), 21.

110 *Our image of God makes us*: Richard Rohr, "A Toxic Image of God,"
     Center for Action and Contemplation newsletter, January 28, 2016.

112 *Our perception of success*: Alice Fryling, *Disciplemakers' Handbook:
     Helping People Grow in Christ* (Downers Grove, IL: InterVarsity Press,
     1989), 64.

113 *Unless the willingness is present*: Thomas Kelly, *A Testament of Devotion*
     (New York: HarperOne, 1996), 21.

8 A Question of Ritual

120 *Just to be is a blessing*: Abraham Heschel, *The Insecurity of Freedom:
     Essays on Human Existence* (New York: Farrar, Strauss, & Giroux,
     1963), 82.

     When we meet a saint: Gordon Smith, *Called to Be Saints: An Invitation
     to Christian Maturity* (Downers Grove, IL: InterVarsity Press, 2014), 19.

121 *One's daily routine*: Mason Currey, *Daily Rituals: How Artists Work*
     (New York: Knopf, 2013), 3.

123   *anything we are "bound" to*: David Dark, *Life's Too Short to Pretend You're Not Religious* (Downers Grove, IL: InterVarsity Press, 2016). This idea is present throughout the book.

    a deep sense of connection: Robert Fulghum, *From Beginning to End: The Rituals of Our Lives* (New York: Ivy Books, 1996), 15.

124   *I cannot take charge*: Eugene Peterson, *Christ Plays in Ten Thousand Places: A Conversation in Spiritual Theology* (Grand Rapids: Eerdmans, 2008), 206.

130   *In a very real sense*: Leighton Ford, *The Attentive Life: Discerning God's Presence in All Things* (Downers Grove, IL: InterVarsity Press, 2014), 36.

    the very essence of our journey to the Center: ibid.

131   *There is a devotion to God*: Emil Brunner, quoted in Craig L. Blomberg, *Matthew*, New American Commentary (Nashville: Holman Reference, 1992), Logos Bible Software.

9 A Question of Forgiveness

137   *Jesus didn't come because all was well*: Kai Nilsen, keynote address, Apprentice Gathering, Friends University, Wichita, KS, October 10, 2015.

140   *vandalism of shalom*: Cornelius Plantinga Jr., *Not the Way It's Supposed to Be: A Breviary of Sin* (Grand Rapids: Eerdmans, 1995), 7.

143   *that fatal capacity for feeling*: Frederick Buechner, quoted in Jones, *Dwell*, 85.

145   *Forgiveness refuses superiority*: David W. Augsburger, *Caring Enough to Forgive: True Forgiveness* (Ventura, CA: Regal, 1981), 108.

146   *colanders of glory water*: Emily Freeman, *A Million Little Ways: Uncovering the Art You Were Made to Live* (Grand Rapids: Revell, 2013), 27-28.

147   *The root of the Hebrew word*: "na-se," *Dictionary of Biblical Languages with Semantic Domains: Hebrew (Old Testament)*, ed. James A. Swanson (Bellingham, WA: FaithLife, 1997), Logos Bible Software, no. 5951.

10 A Question of Change

153 *The spiritual life is not*: Henri Nouwen, *Making All Things New: An Invitation to the Spiritual Life* (New York: HarperOne, 2009), 21.

All shall be well: Julian of Norwich, "Julian of Norwich—Quotes," Goodreads, accessed March 17, 2016, www.goodreads.com/author /quotes/156980.Julian_of_Norwich.

154 *We're all drowning*: Jamie Holmes, *Nonsense: The Power of Not Knowing* (New York: Crown Publishing, 2015), 10.

155 *do what Jesus would do*: Dallas Willard said this in a variety of audio and live talks.

161 *Ronald Rolheiser calls this the difference*: Ronald Rolheiser, *The Holy Longing: The Search for a Christian Spirituality* (New York: Image, 2009), 146.

162 *A pivot occurs when*: Julie Barrios, "Spiritual Formation when Google Fails," *Conversations Journal*, Fall-Winter 2015, 81.

163 *in order to come to fuller life*: Rolheiser, *Holy Longing*, 146.

Grace can never be learned: Sharol Hayner and Steve Hayner, *Joy in the Journey: Finding Abundance in the Shadow of Death* (Downers Grove, IL: InterVarsity Press, 2015), 85.

166 *the inner light*: This concept is talked about thoroughly in Thomas Kelly, *A Testament of Devotion* (New York: HarperOne, 1996).

God did not give: Philip Yancey, *Where Is God When It Hurts?* (Grand Rapids: Zondervan, 1990).

Conclusion

169 *Truth is a not a thought*: Nicholas of Serbia, quoted in George Maksimov, "Three-Hundred Sayings of the Ascetics of the Orthodox Church," Orthodox.cn, January 8, 2011, http://orthodox.cn/patristics/300 sayings_en.htm.

Contact Casey Tygrett

For speaking requests and speaking schedule, go to www.caseytygrett.com.

Facebook: facebook.com/cktygrettauthor

Twitter: @cktygrett // @becomingcurious

Instagram: @cktygrett

formatio
TRADITION. EXPERIENCE.
TRANSFORMATION.

Formatio books from InterVarsity Press follow the rich tradition of the church in the journey of spiritual formation. These books are not merely about being informed, but about being transformed by Christ and conformed to his image. Formatio stands in InterVarsity Press's evangelical publishing tradition by integrating God's Word with spiritual practice and by prompting readers to move from inward change to outward witness. InterVarsity Press uses the chambered nautilus for Formatio, a symbol of spiritual formation because of its continual spiral journey outward as it moves from its center. We believe that each of us is made with a deep desire to be in God's presence. Formatio books help us to fulfill our deepest desires and to become our true selves in light of God's grace.